The Constitution of
The State of New York:
A Quick Reference Guide

Bootblack Budget Books
Copyright 2018 ©
ISBN-13: 978-1719548274
ISBN-10: 1719548277

Contents:

Preamble – Page 28

ARTICLE I: BILL OF RIGHTS – Page 29

Section 1. Rights, Privileges and Franchise Secured; Power of Legislature to Dispense with Primary Elections in Certain Cases

Section 2. Trial by Jury; How Waived

Section 3. Freedom of Worship; Religious Liberty

Section 4. Habeas Corpus

Section 5. Bail; Fines; Punishments; Detention of Witnesses

Section 6. Grand Jury; Protection of Certain Enumerated Rights; Duty of Public Officers to Sign Waiver of Immunity and Give Testimony; Penalty for Refusal

Section 7. Compensation for Taking Private Property; Private Roads; Drainage of Agricultural Lands

Section 8. Freedom of Speech and Press; Criminal Prosecutions for Libel

Section 9. Right to Assemble and Petition; Divorce; Lotteries; Pool-Selling and Gambling; Laws to Prevent; Pari-Mutuel Betting on Horse Races Permitted; Games of Chance, Bingo or Lotto Authorized Under Certain Restrictions

Section 10. Repealed

Section 11. Equal Protection of Laws; Discrimination in Civil Rights Prohibited

Section 12. Security Against Unreasonable Searches, Seizures and Interceptions

Section 13. Repealed

Section 14. Common Law and Acts of the Colonial and State Legislatures

Section 15. Repealed

Section 16. Damages for Injuries Causing Death

Section 17. Labor not a Commodity; Hours and Wages in Public Work; Right to Organize and Bargain Collectively

Section 18. Workers Compensation

ARTICLE II: SUFFRAGE – Page 37

Section 1. Qualifications of Voters

Section 2. Absentee Voting

Section 3. Persons Excluded from the Right of Suffrage

Section 4. Certain Occupations and Conditions not to Affect Residence

Section 5. Registration and Election Laws to be Passed

Section 6. Permanent Registration

Section 7. Manner of Voting; Identification of Voters

Section 8. Bi-Partisan Registration and Election Board

Section 9. Presidential Elections; Special Voting Procedures Authorized

ARTICLE III: LEGISLATURE – Page 41

Section 1. Legislative Power

Section 2. Number and Terms of Senators and Assemblymen

Section 3. Senate Districts

Section 4. Readjustments and Re-Apportionments; When Federal Census to Control

Section 5. Apportionment of Assemblymen; Creation of Assembly Districts

Section 5-A. Definition of Inhabitants

Section 6. Compensation, Allowances and Traveling Expenses of Members

Section 7. Qualifications of Members; Prohibitions on Certain Civil Appointments; Acceptance to Vacate Seat

Section 8. Time of Elections of Members

Section 9. Powers of Each House

Section 10. Journals; Open Sessions; Adjournments

Section 11. Members not to be Questioned for Speeches

Section 12. Bills May Originate in Either House; May be Amended by the Other

Section 13. Enacting Clause of Bills; no Law to be Enacted Except by Bill

Section 14. Manner of Passing Bills; Message of Necessity for Immediate Vote

Section 15. Private or Local Bills to Embrace Only One Subject, Expressed in Title

Section 16. Existing Law not to be Made Applicable by Reference

Section 17. Cases in Which Private or Local Bills Shall not be Passed

Section 18. Extraordinary Sessions of The Legislature; Power to Convene on Legislative Initiative

Section 19. Private Claims not to be Audited by Legislature; Claims Barred by Lapse of Time

Section 20. Two-Thirds Bills

Section 21. Certain Sections not to Apply to Bills Recommended by Certain Commissioners or Public Agencies

Section 22. Tax Laws to State Tax and Object Distinctly; Definition of Income for Income Tax Purposes by Reference to Federal Laws Authorized

Section 23. When Yeas and Nays Necessary; Three-Fifths to Constitute Quorum

Section 24. Prison Labor; Contract System Abolished

Section 25. Emergency Governmental Operations; Legislature to Provide for

ARTICLE IV: EXECUTIVE – Page 64

Section 1. Executive Power; Election and Terms of Governor and Lieutenant-Governor

Section 2. Qualifications of Governor and Lieutenant-Governor

Section 3. Powers and Duties of Governor; Compensation

Section 4. Reprieves, Commutations and Pardons; Powers and Duties of Governor Relating to Grants of

Section 5. When Lieutenant-Governor to Act as Governor

Section 6. Duties and Compensation of Lieutenant-Governor; Succession to the Governorship

Section 7. Action by Governor on Legislative Bills; Reconsideration After Veto

Section 8. Departmental Rules and Regulations; Filing; Publication

ARTICLE V: OFFICERS AND CIVIL DEPARTMENTS – Page 69

Section 1. Comptroller and Attorney-General; Payment of State Moneys Without Audit Void

Section 2. Civil Departments in the State Government

Section 3. Assignment of Functions

Section 4. Department Heads

Section 5. Repealed

Section 6. Civil Service Appointments and Promotions; Veterans' Credits

Section 7. Membership in Retirement Systems; Benefits not to be Diminished nor Impaired

ARTICLE VI: JUDICIARY – Page 74

Section 1. Unified Court System; Organization; Process

Section 2. Court of Appeals; Organization; Designations; Vacancies, How Filled; Commission on Judicial Nomination

Section 3. Court of Appeals; Jurisdiction

Section 4. Judicial Departments; Appellate Divisions, How Constituted; Governor to Designate Justices; Temporary Assignments; Jurisdiction

Section 5. Appeals from Judgment or Order; New Trial

Section 6. Judicial Districts; How Constituted; Supreme Court

Section 7. Supreme Court; Jurisdiction

Section 8. Appellate Terms; Composition; Jurisdiction

Section 9. Court of Claims; Jurisdiction

Section 10. County Courts; Judges

Section 11. County Court; Jurisdiction

Section 12. Surrogate's Courts; Judges; Jurisdiction

Section 13. Family Court; Organization; Jurisdiction

Section 14. Discharge of Duties of More Than One Judicial Office by Same Judicial Officer

Section 15. New York City; City-Wide Courts; Jurisdiction

Section 16. District Courts; Jurisdiction; Judges

Section 17. Town, Village and City Courts; Jurisdiction; Judges

Section 18. Trial by Jury; Trial Without Jury; Claims Against State

Section 19. Transfer of Actions and Proceedings

Section 20. Judges and Justices; Qualifications; Eligibility for Other Office or Service; Restrictions

Section 21. Vacancies; How Filled

Section 22. Commission on Judicial Conduct; Composition; Organization and Procedure; Review by Court of Appeals; Discipline of Judges or Justices

Section 23. Removal of Judges

Section 24. Court for Trial of Impeachments; Judgment

Section 25. Judges and Justices; Compensation; Retirement

Section 26. Temporary Assignments of Judges and Justices

Section 27. Supreme Court; Extraordinary Terms

Section 28. Administrative Supervision of Court System

Section 29. Expenses of Courts

Section 30. Legislative Power Over Jurisdiction and Proceedings; Delegation of Power to Regulate Practice and Procedure

Section 31. Inapplicability of Article to Certain Courts

Section 32. Custodians of Children to be of Same Religious Persuasion

Section 33. Existing Laws; Duty of Legislature to Implement Article

Section 34. Pending Appeals, Actions and Proceedings; Preservation of Existing Terms of Office of Judges and Justices

Section 35. Certain Courts Abolished; Transfer of Judges, Court Personnel, and Actions and Proceedings to Other Courts

Section 36. Pending Civil and Criminal Cases

Section 36-A. Effective Date of Certain Amendments to Articles VI and VII

Section 36-B. No Section

Section 36-C. Effective Date of Certain Amendments to Article VI, Section 22

Section 37. Effective Date of Article

ARTICLE VII: STATE FINANCES – Page 121

Section 1. Estimates by Departments, the Legislature and the Judiciary of Needed Appropriations; Hearings

Section 2. Executive Budget

Section 3. Budget Bills; Appearances Before Legislature

Section 4. Action on Budget Bills by Legislature; Effect Thereof

Section 5. Restrictions on Consideration of Other Appropriations

Section 6. Restrictions on Content of Appropriation Bills

Section 7. Appropriation Bills

Section 8. Gift or Loan of State Credit or Money Prohibited; Exceptions for Enumerated Purposes

Section 9. Short Term State Debts in Anticipation of Taxes, Revenues and Proceeds of Sale of Authorized Bonds

Section 10. State Debts on Account of Invasion, Insurrection, War and Forest Fires

Section 11. State Debts Generally; Manner of Contracting; Referendum

Section 12. State Debts Generally; How Paid; Contribution to Sinking Funds; Restrictions on Use of Bond Proceeds

Section 13. Refund of State Debts

Section 14. State Debt for Elimination of Railroad Crossings at Grade; Expenses; How Borne; Construction and Reconstruction of State Highways and Parkways

Section 15. Sinking Funds; How Kept and Invested; Income Therefrom and Application Thereof

Section 16. Payment of State Debts; When Comptroller to Pay Without Appropriation

Section 17. Authorizing the Legislature to Establish a Fund or Funds for Tax Revenue Stabilization Reserves; Regulating Payments Thereto and Withdrawals Therefrom

Section 18. Bonus on Account of Service of Certain Veterans in World War II

Section 19. State Debt for Expansion of State University

ARTICLE VIII: LOCAL FINANCES – Page 138

Section 1. Gift or Loan of Property or Credit of Local Subdivisions Prohibited; Exceptions for Enumerated Purposes

Section 2. Restrictions of Indebtedness of Local Subdivisions; Contracting and Payment of Local Indebtedness; Exceptions

Section 2-A. Local Indebtedness for Water Supply, Sewage and Drainage Facilities and Purposes; Allocations and Exclusions of Indebtedness

Section 3. Restrictions of Creation and Indebtedness of Certain Corporations

Section 4. Limitations of Local Indebtedness

Section 5. Ascertainment of Debt-Incurring Power of Counties, Cities, Towns and Villages; Certain Indebtedness to be Excluded

Section 6. Debt-Incurring Power of Buffalo, Rochester and Syracuse; Certain Additional Indebtedness to be Excluded

Section 7. Debt-Incurring Power of New York City; Certain Additional Indebtedness to be Excluded

Section 7-A. Debt-Incurring Power of New York City; Certain Indebtedness for Railroads and Transit Purposes to be Excluded

Section 8. Indebtedness Not to be Invalidated By Operation of This Article

Section 9. When Debt-Incurring Power of Certain Counties Shall Cease

Section 10. Limitations of Amount to be Raised By Real Estate Taxes for Local Purposes; Exceptions

Section 10-A. Application and Use of Revenues: Certain Public Improvements

Section 11. Taxes for Certain Capital Expenditures to be Excluded From Tax Limitation

Section 12. Powers of Local Governments to be Restricted; Further Limitations of Contracting Local Indebtedness Authorized

ARTICLE IX: LOCAL GOVERNMENTS – Page 161

Section 1. Bill of Rights for Local Governments

Section 2. Powers and Duties of Legislature; Home Rule Powers of Local Governments; Statute of Local Governments

Section 3. Existing Laws to Remain Applicable; Construction; Definitions

ARTICLE X: CORPORATIONS – Page 168

Section 1. Corporations; Formation of

Section 2. Dues of Corporations

Section 3. Savings Bank Charters; Savings and Loan Association Charters; Special Charters not to be Granted

Section 4. Corporations; Definition; Right to Sue and be Sued

Section 5. Public Corporations; Restrictions on Creation and Powers; Accounts; Obligations of

Section 6. Liability of State For Payment Of Bonds Of Public Corporation To Construct State Thruways; Use Of State Canal Lands And Properties

Section 7. Liability Of State For Obligations Of The Port Of New York Authority For Railroad Commuter Cars; Limitations

Section 8. Liability Of State On Bonds Of A Public Corporation To Finance New Industrial Or Manufacturing Plants In Depressed Areas

ARTICLE XI: EDUCATION – Page 173

Section 1. Common Schools

Section 2. Regents of the University

Section 3. Use of Public Property or Money in Aid of Denominational Schools Prohibited; Transportation of Children Authorized

ARTICLE XII: DEFENSE – Page 174

Section 1. Defense; Militia

ARTICLE XIII: PUBLIC OFFICERS – Page 175

Section 1. Oath of Office; no Other Test for Public Office

Section 2. Duration of Term of Office

Section 3. Vacancies in Office; How Filled; Boards of Education

Section 4. Political Year and Legislative Term

Section 5. Removal from Office for Misconduct

Section 6. When Office to be Deemed Vacant; Legislature May Declare

Section 7. Compensation of Officers

Section 8. Election and Term of City and Certain County Officers

Section 9-12. No Sections 9-12

Section 13. Law Enforcement and Other Officers

Section 14. Employees of, and Contractors for, the State and Local Governments; Wages, Hours and Other Provisions to be Regulated by Legislature

ARTICLE XIV: CONSERVATION – Page 180

Section 1. Forest Preserve to be Forever Kept Wild; Authorized Uses and Exceptions

Section 2. Reservoirs

Section 3. Forest and Wild Life Conservation; Use or Disposition of Certain Lands Authorized

Section 4. Protection of Natural Resources; Development of Agricultural Lands

Section 5. Violations of Article; How Restrained

Section 6. (No Title)

ARTICLE XV: CANALS – Page 189

Section 1. Disposition of Canals and Canal Properties Prohibited

Section 2. Prohibition Inapplicable to Lands and Properties no Longer Useful; Disposition Authorized

Section 3. Contracts for Work and Materials; Special Revenue Fund

Section 4. Lease or Transfer to Federal Government of Barge Canal System Authorized

ARTICLE XVI: TAXATION – Page 192

Section 1. Power of Taxation; Exemptions from Taxation

Section 2. Assessments for Taxation Purposes

Section 3. Situs of Intangible Personal Property; Taxation of

Section 4. Certain Corporations not to be Discriminated Against

Section 5. Compensation of Public Officers and Employees Subject to Taxation

Section 6. Public Improvements or Services; Contract of Indebtedness; Creation of Public Corporations

ARTICLE XVII: SOCIAL WELFARE – Page 195

Section 1. Public relief and care

Section 2. State board of social welfare; powers and duties

Section 3. Public health

Section 4. Care and treatment of persons suffering from mental disorder or defect; visitation of institutions for

Section 5. Institutions for detention of criminals; probation; parole; state commission of correction

Section 6. Visitation and inspection

Section 7. Loans for hospital construction

ARTICLE XVIII: HOUSING – Page 198

Section 1. Housing and Nursing Home Accommodations for Persons of Low Income; Slum Clearance

Section 2. Idem; Powers of Legislature in Aid of

Section 3. Article VII to Apply to State Debts Under this Article, with Certain Exceptions; Amortization of State Debts; Capital and Periodic Subsidies

Section 4. Powers of Cities, Towns and Villages to Contract Indebtedness in Aid of Low Rent Housing and Slum Clearance Projects; Restrictions Thereon

Section 5. Liability for Certain Loans Made by the State to Certain Public Corporations

Section 6. Loans and Subsidies; Restrictions on and Preference in Occupancy of Projects

Section 7. Liability Arising from Guarantees to be Deemed Indebtedness; Method of Computing

Section 8. Excess Condemnation

Section 9. Acquisition of Property for Purposes of Article

Section 10. Power of Legislature; Construction of Article

ARTICLE XIX: AMENDMENTS TO CONSTITUTION – Page 205

Section 1. Amendments to Constitution; How Proposed, Voted Upon and Ratified; Failure of Attorney-General to Render Opinion not to Affect Validity

Section 2. Future Constitutional Conventions; How Called; Election of Delegates; Compensation; Quorum; Submission of Amendments; Officers; Employees; Rules; Vacancies

Section 3. Amendments Simultaneously Submitted by Convention and Legislature

ARTICLE XX: WHEN TO TAKE EFFECT – Page 208

Section 1. Time of Taking Effect

Closing – Page 208

Preamble

We The People of the State of New York, grateful to Almighty God for our Freedom, in order to secure its blessings, DO ESTABLISH THIS CONSTITUTION.

ARTICLE I: BILL OF RIGHTS

Section 1. Rights, Privileges and Franchise Secured; Power of Legislature to Dispense with Primary Elections in Certain Cases

No member of this state shall be disfranchised, or deprived of any of the rights or privileges secured to any citizen thereof, unless by the law of the land, or the judgment of his or her peers, except that the legislature may provide that there shall be no primary election held to nominate candidates for public office or to elect persons to party positions for any political party or parties in any unit of representation of the state from which such candidates or persons are nominated or elected whenever there is no contest or contests for such nominations or election as may be prescribed by general law.

Section 2. Trial by Jury; How Waived

Trial by jury in all cases in which it has heretofore been guaranteed by constitutional provision shall remain inviolate forever; but a jury trial may be waived by the parties in all civil cases in the manner to be prescribed by law. The legislature may provide, however, by law, that a verdict may be rendered by not less than five-sixths of the jury in any civil case. A jury trial may be waived by the defendant in all criminal cases, except those in which the crime charged may be punishable by death, by a written instrument signed by the defendant in person in open court before and with the approval of a judge or justice of a court having jurisdiction to try the offense. The legislature may enact laws, not inconsistent herewith, governing the form, content, manner and time of presentation of the instrument effectuating such waiver.

Section 3. Freedom of Worship; Religious Liberty

The free exercise and enjoyment of religious profession and worship, without discrimination or preference, shall forever be allowed in this state to all humankind; and no person shall be rendered incompetent to be a witness on account of his or her opinions on matters of religious belief; but the liberty of conscience hereby secured shall not be so construed as to excuse acts of licentiousness, or justify practices inconsistent with the peace or safety of this state.

Section 4. Habeas Corpus

The privilege of a writ or order of habeas corpus shall not be suspended, unless, in case of rebellion or invasion, the public safety requires it.

Section 5. Bail; Fines; Punishments; Detention of Witnesses

Excessive bail shall not be required nor excessive fines imposed, nor shall cruel and unusual punishments be inflicted, nor shall witnesses be unreasonably detained.

Section 6. Grand Jury; Protection of Certain Enumerated Rights; Duty of Public Officers to Sign Waiver of Immunity and Give Testimony; Penalty for Refusal

No person shall be held to answer for a capital or otherwise infamous crime (except in cases of impeachment, and in cases of militia when in actual service, and the land, air and naval forces in time of war, or which this state may keep with the consent of congress in time of peace, and in cases of petit larceny under the regulation of the legislature), unless on indictment of a grand jury, except that a person held for the action of a grand jury upon a charge for such an offense, other than one punishable by death or life imprisonment, with the consent of the district attorney, may waive indictment by a grand jury and consent to be prosecuted on an information filed by the district attorney; such waiver shall be evidenced by written instrument signed by the defendant in open court in the presence of his or her counsel. In any trial in any court whatever the party accused shall be allowed to appear and defend in person and with counsel as in civil actions and shall be informed of the nature and cause of the accusation and be confronted with the witnesses against him or her. No person shall be subject to be twice put in jeopardy for the same offense; nor shall he or she be compelled in any criminal case to be a witness against himself or herself, providing, that any public officer who, upon being called before a grand jury to testify concerning the conduct of his or her present office or of any public office held by him or her within five years prior to such grand jury call to testify, or the performance of his or her official duties in any such present or prior offices, refuses to sign a waiver of immunity against subsequent criminal prosecution, or to answer any relevant question concerning such matters before such grand jury, shall by virtue of such refusal, be disqualified from holding any other public office or public employment for a period of five years from the date of such refusal to sign a waiver of immunity against subsequent prosecution, or to answer any relevant question concerning such matters before such grand jury, and shall be removed from his or her present office by the appropriate authority or shall forfeit his or her present office at the suit of the attorney-general.

The power of grand juries to inquire into the wilful misconduct in office of public officers, and to find indictments or to direct the filing of informations in connection with such inquiries, shall never be suspended or impaired by law. No person shall be deprived of life, liberty or property without due process of law.

Section 7. Compensation for Taking Private Property; Private Roads; Drainage of Agricultural Lands

(a) Private property shall not be taken for public use without just compensation.

(c) Private roads may be opened in the manner to be prescribed by law; but in every case the necessity of the road and the amount of all damage to be sustained by the opening thereof shall be first determined by a jury of freeholders, and such amount, together with the expenses of the proceedings, shall be paid by the person to be benefited.

(d) The use of property for the drainage of swamp or agricultural lands is declared to be a public use, and general laws may be passed permitting the owners or occupants of swamp or agricultural lands to construct and maintain for the drainage thereof, necessary drains, ditches and dykes upon the lands of others, under proper restrictions, on making just compensation, and such compensation together with the cost of such drainage may be assessed, wholly or partly, against any property benefited thereby; but no special laws shall be enacted for such purposes.

Section 8. Freedom of Speech and Press; Criminal Prosecutions for Libel

Every citizen may freely speak, write and publish his or her sentiments on all subjects, being responsible for the abuse of that right; and no law shall be passed to restrain or abridge the liberty of speech or of the press. In all criminal prosecutions or indictments for libels, the truth may be given in evidence to the jury; and if it shall appear to the jury that the matter charged as libelous is true, and was published with good motives and for justifiable ends, the party shall be acquitted; and the jury shall have the right to determine the law and the fact.

Section 9. Right to Assemble and Petition; Divorce; Lotteries; Pool-Selling and Gambling; Laws to Prevent; Pari-Mutual Betting on Horse Races Permitted; Games of Chance, Bingo or Lotto Authorized under Certain Restrictions

1. No law shall be passed abridging the rights of the people peaceably to assemble and to petition the government, or any department thereof; nor shall any divorce be granted otherwise than by due judicial proceedings; except as hereinafter provided, no lottery or the sale of lottery tickets, pool- selling, book-making, or any other kind of gambling, except lotteries operated by the state and the sale of lottery tickets in connection therewith as may be authorized and prescribed by the legislature, the net proceeds of which shall be applied exclusively to or in aid or support of education in this state as the legislature may prescribe, except pari-mutual betting on horse races as may be prescribed by the legislature and from which the state shall derive a reasonable revenue for the support of government, and except casino gambling at no more than seven facilities as authorized and prescribed by the legislature shall hereafter be authorized or allowed within this state; and the legislature shall pass appropriate laws to prevent offenses against any of the provisions of this section.

Section 10.

Repealed

Section 11. Equal Protection of Laws; Discrimination in Civil Rights Prohibited

No person shall be denied the equal protection of the laws of this state or any subdivision thereof. No person shall, because of race, color, creed or religion, be subjected to any discrimination in his or her civil rights by any other person or by any firm, corporation, or institution, or by the state or any agency or subdivision of the state.

Section 12. Security Against Unreasonable Searches, Seizures and Interceptions

The right of the people to be secure in their persons, houses, papers and effects, against unreasonable searches and seizures, shall not be violated, and no warrants shall issue, but upon probable cause, supported by oath or affirmation, and particularly describing the place to be searched, and the persons or things to be seized.

The right of the people to be secure against unreasonable interception of telephone and telegraph communications shall not be violated, and ex parte orders or warrants shall issue only upon oath or affirmation that there is reasonable ground to believe that evidence of crime may be thus obtained, and identifying the particular means of communication, and particularly describing the person or persons whose communications are to be intercepted and the purpose thereof.

Section 13.

Repealed

Section 14. Common Law and Acts of the Colonial and State Legislatures

Such parts of the common law, and of the acts of the legislature of the colony of New York, as together did form the law of the said colony, on the nineteenth day of April, one thousand seven hundred seventy-five, and the resolutions of the congress of the said colony, and of the convention of the State of New York, in force on the twentieth day of April, one thousand seven hundred seventy-seven, which have not since expired, or been repealed or altered; and such acts of the legislature of this state as are now in force, shall be and continue the law of this state, subject to such alterations as the legislature shall make concerning the same. But all such parts of the common law, and such of the said acts, or parts thereof, as are repugnant to this constitution, are hereby abrogated.

Section 15.

Repealed

Section 16. Damages for Injuries Causing Death

The right of action now existing to recover damages for injuries resulting in death, shall never be abrogated; and the amount recoverable shall not be subject to any statutory limitation.
Amendments

Section 17. Labor Not a Commodity; Hours and Wages in Public Work; Right to Organize and Bargain Collectively

Labor of human beings is not a commodity nor an article of commerce and shall never be so considered or construed.
No laborer, worker or mechanic, in the employ of a contractor or sub-contractor engaged in the performance of any public work, shall be permitted to work more than eight hours in any day or more than five days in any week, except in cases of extraordinary emergency; nor shall he or she be paid less than the rate of wages prevailing in the same trade or occupation in the locality within the state where such public work is to be situated, erected or used.

Employees shall have the right to organize and to bargain collectively through representatives of their own choosing.

Section 18. Worker's Compensation

Nothing contained in this constitution shall be construed to limit the power of the legislature to enact laws for the protection of the lives, health, or safety of employees; or for the payment, either by employers, or by employers and employees or otherwise, either directly or through a state or other system of insurance or otherwise, of compensation for injuries to employees or for death of employees resulting from such injuries without regard to fault as a cause thereof, except where the injury is occasioned by the wilful intention of the injured employee to bring about the injury or death of himself or herself or of another, or where the injury results solely from the intoxication of the injured employee while on duty; or for the adjustment, determination and settlement, with or without trial by jury, of issues which may arise under such legislation; or to provide that the right of such compensation, and the remedy therefore shall be exclusive of all other rights and remedies for injuries to employees or for death resulting from such injuries; or to provide that the amount of such compensation for death shall not exceed a fixed or determinable sum; provided that all moneys paid by an employer to his or her employees or their legal representatives, by reason of the enactment of any of the laws herein authorized, shall be held to be a proper charge in the cost of operating the business of the employer.

ARTICLE II: SUFFRAGE

Section 1. Qualifications of Voters

Every citizen shall be entitled to vote at every election for all officers elected by the people and upon all questions submitted to the vote of the people provided that such citizen is eighteen years of age or over and shall have been a resident of this state, and of the county, city, or village for thirty days next preceding an election.

Section 2. Absentee Voting

The legislature may, by general law, provide a manner in which, and the time and place at which, qualified voters who, on the occurrence of any election, may be absent from the county of their residence or, if residents of the city of New York, from the city, and qualified voters who, on the occurrence of any election, may be unable to appear personally at the polling place because of illness or physical disability, may vote and for the return and canvass of their votes.

Section 3. Persons Excluded from the Right of Suffrage

No person who shall receive, accept, or offer to receive, or pay, offer or promise to pay, contribute, offer or promise to contribute to another, to be paid or used, any money or other valuable thing as a compensation or reward for the giving or withholding a vote at an election, or who shall make any promise to influence the giving or withholding any such vote, or who shall make or become directly or indirectly interested in any bet or wager depending upon the result of any election, shall vote at such election; and upon challenge for such cause, the person so challenged, before the officers authorized for that purpose shall receive his or her vote, shall swear or affirm before such officers that he or she has not received or offered, does not expect to receive, has not paid, offered or promised to pay, contributed, offered or promised to contribute to another, to be paid or used, any money or other valuable thing as a compensation or reward for the giving or withholding a vote at such election, and has not made any promise to influence the giving or withholding of any such vote, nor made or become directly or indirectly interested in any bet or wager depending upon the result of such election. The legislature shall enact laws excluding from the right of suffrage all persons convicted of bribery or of any infamous crime.

Section 4. Certain Occupations and Conditions Not to Affect Residence

For the purpose of voting, no person shall be deemed to have gained or lost a residence, by reason of his or her presence or absence, while employed in the service of the United States; nor while engaged in the navigation of the waters of this state, or of the United States, or of the high seas; nor while a student of any seminary of learning; nor while kept at any almshouse, or other asylum, or institution wholly or partly supported at public expense or by charity; nor while confined in any public prison.

Section 5. Registration and Election Laws to Be Passed

Laws shall be made for ascertaining, by proper proofs, the citizens who shall be entitled to the right of suffrage hereby established, and for the registration of voters; which registration shall be completed at least ten days before each election. Such registration shall not be required for town and village elections except by express provision of law.

Section 6. Permanent Registration

The legislature may provide by law for a system or systems of registration whereby upon personal application a voter may be registered and his or her registration continued so long as he or she shall remain qualified to vote from an address within the jurisdiction of the board with which such voter is registered.

Section 7. Manner of Voting; Identification of Voters

All elections by the citizens, except for such town officers as may by law be directed to be otherwise chosen, shall be by ballot, or by such other method as may be prescribed by law, provided that secrecy in voting be preserved. The legislature shall provide for identification of voters through their signatures in all cases where personal registration is required and shall also provide for the signatures, at the time of voting, of all persons voting in person by ballot or voting machine, whether or not they have registered in person, save only in cases of illiteracy or physical disability.

Section 8. Bi-Partisan Registration and Election Boards

All laws creating, regulating or affecting boards or officers charged with the duty of qualifying voters, or of distributing ballots to voters, or of receiving, recording or counting votes at elections, shall secure equal representation of the two political parties which, at the general election next preceding that for which such boards or officers are to serve, cast the highest and the next highest number of votes. All such boards and officers shall be appointed or elected in such manner, and upon the nomination of such representatives of said parties respectively, as the legislature may direct. Existing laws on this subject shall continue until the legislature shall otherwise provide. This section shall not apply to town, or village elections.

Section 9. Presidential Elections; Special Voting Procedures Authorized

Notwithstanding the residence requirements imposed by section one of this article, the legislature may, by general law, provide special procedures whereby every person who shall have moved from another state to this state or from one county, city or village within this state to another county, city or village within this state and who shall have been an inhabitant of this state in any event for ninety days next preceding an election at which electors are to be chosen for the office of president and vice president of the United States shall be entitled to vote in this state solely for such electors, provided such person is otherwise qualified to vote in this state and is not able to qualify to vote for such electors in any other state. The legislature may also, by general law, prescribe special procedures whereby every person who is registered and would be qualified to vote in this state but for his or her removal from this state to another state within one year next preceding such election shall be entitled to vote in this state solely for such electors, provided such person is not able to qualify to vote for such electors in any other state.

ARTICLE III: LEGISLATURE

Section 1. Legislative Power

The legislative power of this state shall be vested in the senate and assembly.

Section 2. Number and Terms of Senators and Assemblymen

The senate shall consist of fifty members,* except as hereinafter provided. The senators elected in the year one thousand eight hundred and ninety-five shall hold their offices for three years, and their successors shall be chosen for two years. The assembly shall consist of one hundred and fifty members. The assembly members elected in the year one thousand nine hundred and thirty-eight, and their successors, shall be chosen for two years.

Section 3. Senate Districts

The senate districts described in section three of article three of this constitution as adopted by the people on November sixth, eighteen hundred ninety-four are hereby continued for all of the purposes of future reapportionments of senate districts pursuant to section four of this article.

Section 4. Readjustments and Reapportionments; When Federal Census to Control

(a) Except as herein otherwise provided, the federal census taken in the year nineteen hundred thirty and each federal census taken decennially thereafter shall be controlling as to the number of inhabitants in the state or any part thereof for the purposes of the apportionment of members of assembly and readjustment or alteration of senate and assembly districts next occurring, in so far as such census and the tabulation thereof purport to give the information necessary therefore. The legislature, by law, shall provide for the making and tabulation by state authorities of an enumeration of the inhabitants of the entire state to be used for such purposes, instead of a federal census, if the taking of a federal census in any tenth year from the year nineteen hundred thirty be omitted or if the federal census fails to show the number of aliens or Indians not taxed. If a federal census, though giving the requisite information as to the state at large, fails to give the information as to any civil or territorial divisions which is required to be known for such purposes, the legislature, by law, shall provide for such an enumeration of the inhabitants of such parts of the state only as may be necessary, which shall supersede in part the federal census and be used in connection therewith for such purposes. The legislature, by law, may provide in its discretion for an enumeration by state authorities of the inhabitants of the state, to be used for such purposes, in place of a federal census, when the return of a decennial federal census is delayed so that it is not available at the beginning of the regular session of the legislature in the second year after the year nineteen hundred thirty or after any tenth year therefrom, or if an apportionment of members of assembly and readjustment or alteration of senate districts is not made at or before such a session. At the regular session in the year nineteen hundred thirty-two, and at the first regular session after the year nineteen hundred forty and after each tenth year therefrom the senate districts shall be readjusted or altered, but if, in any decade, counting from and including that which begins with the year nineteen hundred thirty-one, such a readjustment or alteration is not made at the time above prescribed, it shall be made at a subsequent session occurring not later than the sixth year of such decade, meaning not later than nineteen hundred thirty-six, nineteen hundred forty-six, nineteen hundred fifty-six, and so on; provided, however, that if such districts shall have been readjusted or altered by law in either of the years nineteen hundred thirty or nineteen hundred thirty-one, they shall remain unaltered until the first regular session after the year nineteen hundred forty. No town, except a town having more than a full ratio of apportionment, and no block in a city inclosed by streets or public ways, shall be divided in the formation of senate districts. In the reapportionment of senate districts, no district shall contain a greater excess in population over an adjoining district in the same county, than the population of a town or block therein adjoining such district. Counties, towns or blocks which, from their location, may be included in either of two districts, shall be so placed as to make said districts most nearly equal in number of inhabitants, excluding aliens.

No county shall have four or more senators unless it shall have a full ratio for each senator. No county shall have more than one-third of all the senators; and no two counties or the territory thereof as now organized, which are adjoining counties, or which are separated only by public waters, shall have more than one-half of all the senators.

(b) The independent redistricting commission established pursuant to section five-b of this article shall prepare a redistricting plan to establish senate, assembly, and congressional districts every ten years commencing in two thousand twenty-one, and shall submit to the legislature such plan and the implementing legislation therefor on or before January first or as soon as practicable thereafter but no later than January fifteenth in the year ending in two beginning in two thousand twenty-two. The redistricting plans for the assembly and the senate shall be contained in and voted upon by the legislature in a single bill, and the congressional district plan may be included in the same bill if the legislature chooses to do so. The implementing legislation shall be voted upon, without amendment, by the senate or the assembly and if approved by the first house voting upon it, such legislation shall be delivered to the other house immediately to be voted upon without amendment. If approved by both houses, such legislation shall be presented to the governor for action.

If either house shall fail to approve the legislation implementing the first redistricting plan, or the governor shall veto such legislation and the legislature shall fail to override such veto, each house or the governor if he or she vetoes it, shall notify the commission that such legislation has been disapproved. Within fifteen days of such notification and in no case later than

February twenty-eighth, the redistricting commission shall prepare and submit to the legislature a second redistricting plan and the necessary implementing legislation for such plan. Such legislation shall be voted upon, without amendment, by the senate or the assembly and, if approved by the first house voting upon it, such legislation shall be delivered to the other house immediately to be voted upon without amendment. If approved by both houses, such legislation shall be presented to the governor for action.

If either house shall fail to approve the legislation implementing the second redistricting plan, or the governor shall veto such legislation and the legislature shall fail to override such veto, each house shall introduce such implementing legislation with any amendments each house of the legislature deems necessary. All such amendments shall comply with the provisions of this article. If approved by both houses, such legislation shall be presented to the governor for action.

All votes by the senate or assembly on any redistricting plan legislation pursuant to this article shall be conducted in accordance with the following rules:

(1) In the event that the speaker of the assembly and the temporary president of the senate are members of two different political parties, approval of legislation submitted by the independent redistricting commission pursuant to subdivision (f) of section five-b of this article shall require the vote in support of its passage by at least a majority of the members elected to each house.

(2) In the event that the speaker of the assembly and the temporary president of the senate are members of two different political parties, approval of legislation submitted by the independent redistricting commission pursuant to subdivision (g) of section five-b of this article shall require the vote in support of its passage by at least sixty percent of the members elected to each house.

(3) In the event that the speaker of the assembly and the temporary president of the senate are members of the same political party, approval of legislation submitted by the independent redistricting commission pursuant to subdivision (f) or (g) of section five-b of this article shall require the vote in support of its passage by at least two-thirds of the members elected to each house.

(c) Subject to the requirements of the federal constitution and statutes and in compliance with state constitutional requirements, the following principles shall be used in the creation of state senate and state assembly districts and congressional districts:

(1) When drawing district lines, the commission shall consider whether such lines would result in the denial or abridgement of racial or language minority voting rights, and districts shall not be drawn to have the purpose of, nor shall they result in, the denial or abridgement of such rights. Districts shall be drawn so that, based on the totality of the circumstances, racial or minority language groups do not have less opportunity to participate in the political process than other members of the electorate and to elect representatives of their choice.

(2) To the extent practicable, districts shall contain as nearly as may be an equal number of inhabitants. For each district that deviates from this requirement, the commission shall provide a specific public explanation as to why such deviation exists.

(3) Each district shall consist of contiguous territory.

(4) Each district shall be as compact in form as practicable.

(5) Districts shall not be drawn to discourage competition or for the purpose of favoring or disfavoring incumbents or other particular candidates or political parties. The commission shall consider the maintenance of cores of existing districts, of pre-existing political subdivisions, including counties, cities, and towns, and of communities of interest.

(6) In drawing senate districts, towns or blocks which, from their location may be included in either of two districts, shall be so placed as to make said districts most nearly equal in number of inhabitants. The requirements that senate districts not divide counties or towns, as well as the 'block-on-border' and 'town-on-border' rules, shall remain in effect.

During the preparation of the redistricting plan, the independent redistricting commission shall conduct not less than one public hearing on proposals for the redistricting of congressional and state legislative districts in each of the following (i) cities: Albany, Buffalo, Syracuse, Rochester, and White Plains; and (ii) counties: Bronx, Kings, New York, Queens, Richmond, Nassau, and Suffolk. Notice of all such hearings shall be widely published using the best available means and media a reasonable time before every hearing. At least thirty days prior to the first public hearing and in any event no later than September fifteenth of the year ending in one or as soon as practicable thereafter, the independent redistricting commission shall make widely available to the public, in print form and using the best available technology, its draft redistricting plans, relevant data, and related information. Such plans, data, and information shall be in a form that allows and facilitates their use by the public to review, analyze, and comment upon such plans and to develop alternative redistricting plans for presentation to the commission at the public hearings. The independent redistricting commission shall report the findings of all such hearings to the legislature upon submission of a redistricting plan.

(d) The ratio for apportioning senators shall always be obtained by dividing the number of inhabitants, excluding aliens, by fifty, and the senate shall always be composed of fifty members, except that if any county having three or more senators at the time of any apportionment shall be entitled on such ratio to an additional senator or senators, such additional senator or senators shall be given to such county in addition to the fifty senators, and the whole number of senators shall be increased to that extent.

The senate districts, including the present ones, as existing immediately before the enactment of a law readjusting or altering the senate districts, shall continue to be the senate districts of the state until the expirations of the terms of the senators then in office, except for the purpose of an election of senators for full terms beginning at such expirations, and for the formation of assembly districts.

(e) The process for redistricting congressional and state legislative districts established by this section and sections five and five-b of this article shall govern redistricting in this state except to the extent that a court is required to order the adoption of, or changes to, a redistricting plan as a remedy for a violation of law. A reapportionment plan and the districts contained in such plan shall be in force until the effective date of a plan based upon the subsequent federal decennial census taken in a year ending in zero unless modified pursuant to court order.

Section 5. Apportionment of Assemblymen; Creation of Assembly Districts

The members of the assembly shall be chosen by single districts and shall be apportioned pursuant to this section and sections four and five-b of this article at each regular session at which the senate districts are readjusted or altered, and by the same law, among the several counties of the state, as nearly as may be according to the number of their respective inhabitants, excluding aliens. Every county heretofore established and separately organized, except the county of Hamilton, shall always be entitled to one member of assembly, and no county shall hereafter be erected unless its population shall entitle it to a member. The county of Hamilton shall elect with the county of Fulton, until the population of the county of Hamilton shall, according to the ratio, entitle it to a member. But the legislature may abolish the said county of Hamilton and annex the territory thereof to some other county or counties.

The quotient obtained by dividing the whole number of inhabitants of the state, excluding aliens, by the number of members of assembly, shall be the ratio for apportionment, which shall be made as follows: One member of assembly shall be apportioned to every county, including Fulton and Hamilton as one county, containing less than the ratio and one-half over. Two members shall be apportioned to every other county. The remaining members of assembly shall be apportioned to the counties having more than two ratios according to the number of inhabitants, excluding aliens. Members apportioned on remainders shall be apportioned to the counties having the highest remainders in the order thereof respectively. No county shall have more members of assembly than a county having a greater number of inhabitants, excluding aliens.

The assembly districts, including the present ones, as existing immediately before the enactment of a law making an apportionment of members of assembly among the counties, shall continue to be the assembly districts of the state until the expiration of the terms of members then in office, except for the purpose of an election of members of assembly for full terms beginning at such expirations.

In any county entitled to more than one member, the board of supervisors, and in any city embracing an entire county and having no board of supervisors, the common council, or if there be none, the body exercising the powers of a common council, shall assemble at such times as the legislature making an apportionment shall prescribe, and divide such counties into assembly districts as nearly equal in number of inhabitants, excluding aliens, as may be, of convenient and contiguous territory in as compact form as practicable, each of which shall be wholly within a senate district formed under the same apportionment, equal to the number of members of assembly to which such county shall be entitled, and shall cause to be filed in

the office of the secretary of state and of the clerk of such county, a description of such districts, specifying the number of each district and of the inhabitants thereof, excluding aliens, according to the census or enumeration used as the population basis for the formation of such districts; and such apportionment and districts shall remain unaltered until after the next reapportionment of members of assembly, except that the board of supervisors of any county containing a town having more than a ratio of apportionment and one-half over may alter the assembly districts in a senate district containing such town at any time on or before March first, nineteen hundred forty-six. In counties having more than one senate district, the same number of assembly districts shall be put in each senate district, unless the assembly districts cannot be evenly divided among the senate districts of any county, in which case one more assembly district shall be put in the senate district in such county having the largest, or one less assembly district shall be put in the senate district in such county having the smallest number of inhabitants, excluding aliens, as the case may require. Nothing in this section shall prevent the division, at any time, of counties and towns and the erection of new towns by the legislature.
An apportionment by the legislature, or other body, shall be subject to review by the supreme court, at the suit of any citizen, under such reasonable regulations as the legislature may prescribe; and any court before which a cause may be pending involving an apportionment, shall give precedence thereto over all other causes and proceedings, and if said court be not in session it shall convene promptly for the disposition of the same. The court shall render its decision within sixty days after a petition is filed. In any judicial proceeding relating to redistricting of congressional or state legislative districts, any law establishing congressional or state legislative districts found to violate the provisions of this article shall be invalid in whole or in part. In the event that a court finds such a violation, the legislature shall have a full and reasonable opportunity to correct the law's legal infirmities.

Section 5-a. Definition of Inhabitants

For the purpose of apportioning senate and assembly districts pursuant to the foregoing provisions of this article, the term "inhabitants, excluding aliens" shall mean the whole number of persons.

Section 5-b.

(a) On or before February first of each year ending with a zero and at any other time a court orders that congressional or state legislative districts be amended, an independent redistricting commission shall be established to determine the district lines for congressional and state legislative offices. The independent redistricting commission shall be composed of ten members, appointed as follows:

(1) two members shall be appointed by the temporary president of the senate;

(2) two members shall be appointed by the speaker of the assembly;

(3) two members shall be appointed by the minority leader of the senate;

(4) two members shall be appointed by the minority leader of the assembly;

(5) two members shall be appointed by the eight members appointed pursuant to paragraphs (1) through (4) of this subdivision by a vote of not less than five members in favor of such appointment, and these two members shall not have been enrolled in the preceding five years in either of the two political parties that contain the largest or second largest number of enrolled voters within the state;

(6) one member shall be designated chair of the commission by a majority of the members appointed pursuant to paragraphs (1) through (5) of this subdivision to convene and preside over each meeting of the commission.

(b) The members of the independent redistricting commission shall be registered voters in this state. No member shall within the last three years:

(1) be or have been a member of the New York state legislature or United States Congress or a statewide elected official;

(2) be or have been a state officer or employee or legislative employee as defined in section seventy- three of the public officers law;

(3) be or have been a registered lobbyist in New York state;

(4) be or have been a political party chairman, as defined in paragraph (k) of subdivision one of section seventy-three of the public officers law;

(5) be the spouse of a statewide elected official or of any member of the United States Congress, or of the state legislature.

(c) To the extent practicable, the members of the independent redistricting commission shall reflect the diversity of the residents of this state with regard to race, ethnicity, gender, language, and geographic residence and to the extent practicable the appointing authorities shall consult with organizations devoted to protecting the voting rights of minority and other voters concerning potential appointees to the commission.

(d) Vacancies in the membership of the commission shall be filled within thirty days in the manner provided for in the original appointments.

(e) The legislature shall provide by law for the compensation of the members of the independent redistricting commission, including compensation for actual and necessary expenses incurred in the performance of their duties.

(f) A minimum of five members of the independent redistricting commission shall constitute a quorum for the transaction of any business or the exercise of any power of such commission prior to the appointment of the two commission members appointed pursuant to paragraph (5) of subdivision (a) of this section, and a minimum of seven members shall constitute a quorum after such members have been appointed, and no exercise of any power of the independent redistricting commission shall occur without the affirmative vote of at least a majority of the members, provided that, in order to approve any redistricting plan and implementing legislation, the following rules shall apply:

(1) In the event that the speaker of the assembly and the temporary president of the senate are members of the same political party, approval of a redistricting plan and implementing legislation by the commission for submission to the legislature shall require the vote in support of its approval by at least seven members including at least one member appointed by each of the legislative leaders.

(2) In the event that the speaker of the assembly and the temporary president of the senate are members of two different political parties, approval of a redistricting plan by the commission for submission to the legislature shall require the vote in support of its approval by at least seven members including at least one member appointed by the speaker of the assembly and one member appointed by the temporary president of the senate.

(g) In the event that the commission is unable to obtain seven votes to approve a redistricting plan on or before January first in the year ending in two or as soon as practicable thereafter, the commission shall submit to the legislature that redistricting plan and implementing legislation that garnered the highest number of votes in support of its approval by the commission with a record of the votes taken. In the event that more than one plan received the same number of votes for approval, and such number was higher than that for any other plan, then the commission shall submit all plans that obtained such number of votes. The legislature shall consider and vote upon such implementing legislation in accordance with the voting rules set forth in subdivision (b) of section four of this article.

(h) (1) The independent redistricting commission shall appoint two co-executive directors by a majority vote of the commission in accordance with the following procedure:

(i) In the event that the speaker of the assembly and the temporary president of the senate are members of two different political parties, the co-executive directors shall be approved by a majority of the commission that includes at least one appointee by the speaker of the assembly and at least one appointee by the temporary president of the senate.

(ii) In the event that the speaker of the assembly and the temporary president of the senate are members of the same political party, the co-executive directors shall be approved by a majority of the commission that includes at least one appointee by each of the legislative leaders.

(2) One of the co-executive directors shall be enrolled in the political party with the highest number of enrolled members in the state and one shall be enrolled in the political party with the second highest number of enrolled members in the state. The co-executive directors shall appoint such staff as are necessary to perform the commission's duties, except that the commission shall review a staffing plan prepared and provided by the co-executive directors which shall contain a list of the various positions and the duties, qualifications, and salaries associated with each position.

(3) In the event that the commission is unable to appoint one or both of the co-executive directors within forty-five days of the establishment of a quorum of seven commissioners, the following procedure shall be followed:

(i) In the event that the speaker of the assembly and the temporary president of the senate are members of two different political parties, within ten days the speaker's appointees on the commission shall appoint one co-executive director, and the temporary president's appointees on the commission shall appoint the other co-executive director. Also within ten days the minority leader of the assembly shall select a co-deputy executive director, and the minority leader of the senate shall select the other co-deputy executive director.

(ii) In the event that the speaker of the assembly and the temporary president of the senate are members of the same political party, within ten days the speaker's and temporary president's appointees on the commission shall together appoint one co-executive director, and the two minority leaders' appointees on the commission shall together appoint the other co-executive director.

(4) In the event of a vacancy in the offices of co-executive director or co-deputy executive director, the position shall be filled within ten days of its occurrence by the same appointing authority or authorities that appointed his or her predecessor.

(i) The state budget shall include necessary appropriations for the expenses of the independent redistricting commission, provide for compensation and reimbursement of expenses for the members and staff of the commission, assign to the commission any additional duties that the legislature may deem necessary to the performance of the duties stipulated in this article, and require other agencies and officials of the state of New York and its political subdivisions to provide such information and assistance as the commission may require to perform its duties.

Section 6. Compensation, Allowances and Traveling Expenses of Members

Each member of the legislature shall receive for his or her services a like annual salary, to be fixed by law. He or she shall also be reimbursed for his or her actual traveling expenses in going to and returning from the place in which the legislature meets, not more than once each week while the legislature is in session. Senators, when the senate alone is convened in extraordinary session, or when serving as members of the court for the trial of impeachments, and such members of the assembly, not exceeding nine in number, as shall be appointed managers of an impeachment, shall receive an additional per diem allowance, to be fixed by law. Any member, while serving as an officer of his or her house or in any other special capacity therein or directly connected therewith not hereinbefore in this section specified, may also be paid and receive, in addition, any allowance which may be fixed by law for the particular and additional services appertaining to or entailed by such office or special capacity. Neither the salary of any member nor any other allowance so fixed may be increased or diminished during, and with respect to, the term for which he or she shall have been elected, nor shall he or she be paid or receive any other extra compensation. The provisions of this section and laws enacted in compliance therewith shall govern and be exclusively controlling, according to their terms. Members shall continue to receive such salary and additional allowance as heretofore fixed and provided in this section, until changed by law pursuant to this section.

Section 7. Qualifications of Members; Prohibitions on Certain Civil Appointments; Acceptance to Vacate Seat

No person shall serve as a member of the legislature unless he or she is a citizen of the United States and has been a resident of the state of New York for five years, and, except as hereinafter otherwise prescribed, of the assembly or senate district for the twelve months immediately preceding his or her election; if elected a senator or member of assembly at the first election next ensuing after a readjustment or alteration of the senate or assembly districts becomes effective, a person, to be eligible to serve as such, must have been a resident of the county in which the senate or assembly district is contained for the twelve months immediately preceding his or her election. No member of the legislature shall, during the time for which he or she was elected, receive any civil appointment from the governor, the governor and the senate, the legislature or from any city government, to an office which shall have been created, or the emoluments whereof shall have been increased during such time. If a member of the legislature be elected to congress, or appointed to any office, civil or military, under the government of the United States, the state of New York, or under any city government except as a member of the national guard or naval militia of the state, or of the reserve forces of the United States, his or her acceptance thereof shall vacate his or her seat in the legislature, providing, however, that a member of the legislature may be appointed commissioner of deeds or to any office in which he or she shall receive no compensation.

Section 8. Time of Elections of Members

The elections of senators and members of assembly, pursuant to the provisions of this constitution, shall be held on the Tuesday succeeding the first Monday of November, unless otherwise directed by the legislature.

Section 9. Powers of Each House

A majority of each house shall constitute a quorum to do business. Each house shall determine the rules of its own proceedings, and be the judge of the elections, returns and qualifications of its own members; shall choose its own officers; and the senate shall choose a temporary president and the assembly shall choose a speaker.

Section 10. Journals; Open Sessions; Adjournments

Each house of the legislature shall keep a journal of its proceedings, and publish the same, except such parts as may require secrecy. The doors of each house shall be kept open, except when the public welfare shall require secrecy. Neither house shall, without the consent of the other, adjourn for more than two days.

Section 11. Members Not to Be Questioned for Speeches

For any speech or debate in either house of the legislature, the members shall not be questioned in any other place.

Section 12. Bills May Originate in Either House; May Be Amended by the Other

Any bill may originate in either house of the legislature, and all bills passed by one house may be amended by the other.

Section 13. Enacting Clause of Bills; No Law to Be Enacted Except by Bill

The enacting clause of all bills shall be "The People of the State of New York, represented in Senate and Assembly, do enact as follows," and no law shall be enacted except by bill.

Section 14. Manner of Passing Bills; Message of Necessity for Immediate Vote

No bill shall be passed or become a law unless it shall have been printed and upon the desks of the members, in its final form, at least three calendar legislative days prior to its final passage, unless the governor, or the acting governor, shall have certified, under his or her hand and the seal of the state, the facts which in his or her opinion necessitate an immediate vote thereon, in which case it must nevertheless be upon the desks of the members in final form, not necessarily printed, before its final passage; nor shall any bill be passed or become a law, except by the assent of a majority of the members elected to each branch of the legislature; and upon the last reading of a bill, no amendment thereof shall be allowed, and the question upon its final passage shall be taken immediately thereafter, and the ayes and nays entered on the journal.

For purposes of this section, a bill shall be deemed to be printed and upon the desks of the members if: it is set forth in a legible electronic format by electronic means, and it is available for review in such format at the desks of the members. For the purposes of this section "electronic means" means any method of transmission of information between computers or other machines designed for the purpose of sending and receiving such transmissions and which: allows the recipient to reproduce the information transmitted in a tangible medium of expression; and does not permit additions, deletions or other changes to be made without leaving an adequate record thereof.

Section 15. Private or Local Bills to Embrace Only One Subject, Expressed in Title

No private or local bill, which may be passed by the legislature, shall embrace more than one subject, and that shall be expressed in the title.

Section 16. Existing Law Not to Be Made Applicable by Reference

No act shall be passed which shall provide that any existing law, or any part thereof, shall be made or deemed a part of said act, or which shall enact that any existing law, or part thereof, shall be applicable, except by inserting it in such act.

Section 17. Cases in which Private or Local Bills Shall Not Be Passed

The legislature shall not pass a private or local bill in any of the following cases:

Changing the names of persons.

Laying out, opening, altering, working or discontinuing roads, highways or alleys, or for draining swamps or other low lands.

Locating or changing county seats.
Providing for changes of venue in civil or criminal cases.

Incorporating villages.

Providing for election of members of boards of supervisors.

Selecting, drawing, summoning or empaneling grand or petit jurors.

Regulating the rate of interest on money.

The opening and conducting of elections or designating places of voting.

Creating, increasing or decreasing fees, percentages or allowances of public officers, during the term for which said officers are elected or appointed.

Granting to any corporation, association or individual the right to lay down railroad tracks.

Granting to any private corporation, association or individual any exclusive privilege, immunity or franchise whatever.

Granting to any person, association, firm or corporation, an exemption from taxation on real or personal property.

Providing for the building of bridges, except over the waters forming a part of the boundaries of the state, by other than a municipal or other public corporation or a public agency of the state.

Section 18. Extraordinary Sessions of the Legislature; Power to Convene on Legislative Initiative

The members of the legislature shall be empowered, upon the presentation to the temporary president of the senate and the speaker of the assembly of a petition signed by two-thirds of the members elected to each house of the legislature, to convene the legislature on extraordinary occasions to act upon the subjects enumerated in such petition.

Section 19. Private Claims Not to Be Audited by Legislature; Claims Barred by Lapse of Time

The legislature shall neither audit nor allow any private claim or account against the state, but may appropriate money to pay such claims as shall have been audited and allowed according to law.

No claim against the state shall be audited, allowed or paid which, as between citizens of the state, would be barred by lapse of time. But if the claimant shall be under legal disability, the claim may be presented within two years after such disability is removed.

Section 20. Two-Thirds Bills

The assent of two-thirds of the members elected to each branch of the legislature shall be requisite to every bill appropriating the public moneys or property for local or private purposes.

Section 21. Certain Sections Not to Apply to Bills Recommended by Certain Commissioners or Public Agencies

Sections 15, 16 and 17 of this article shall not apply to any bill, or the amendments to any bill, which shall be recommended to the legislature by commissioners or any public agency appointed or directed pursuant to law to prepare revisions, consolidations or compilations of statutes. But a bill amending an existing law shall not be excepted from the provisions of sections 15, 16 and 17 of this article unless such amending bill shall itself be recommended to the legislature by such commissioners or public agency.

Section 22. Tax Laws to State Tax and Object Distinctly; Definition of Income for Income Tax Purposes by Reference to Federal Laws Authorized

Every law which imposes, continues or revives a tax shall distinctly state the tax and the object to which it is to be applied, and it shall not be sufficient to refer to any other law to fix such tax or object.

Notwithstanding the foregoing or any other provision of this constitution, the legislature, in any law imposing a tax or taxes on, in respect to or measured by income, may define the income on, in respect to or by which such tax or taxes are imposed or measured, by reference to any provision of the laws of the United States as the same may be or become effective at any time or from time to time, and may prescribe exceptions or modifications to any such provision.

Section 23. When Yeas and Nays Necessary; Three-Fifths to Constitute Quorum

On the final passage, in either house of the legislature, of any act which imposes, continues or revives a tax, or creates a debt or charge, or makes, continues or revives any appropriation of public or trust money or property, or releases, discharges or commutes any claim or demand of the state, the question shall be taken by yeas and nays, which shall be duly entered upon the journals, and three-fifths of all the members elected to either house shall, in all such cases, be necessary to constitute a quorum therein.

Section 24. Prison Labor; Contract System Abolished

The legislature shall, by law, provide for the occupation and employment of prisoners sentenced to the several state prisons, penitentiaries, jails and reformatories in the state; and no person in any such prison, penitentiary, jail or reformatory, shall be required or allowed to work, while under sentence thereto, at any trade, industry or occupation, wherein or whereby his or her work, or the product or profit of his or her work, shall be farmed out, contracted, given or sold to any person, firm, association or corporation, provided that the legislature may provide by law that such prisoners may voluntarily perfrom work for nonprofit organizations. As used in this section, the terms "nonprofit organization means an organization operated exclusively for religious, charitable, or educational purposes, no part of the net earnings of which inures to the benefit of any private shareholder or individual. This section shall not be construed to prevent the legislature from providing that convicts may work for, and that the products of their labor may be disposed of to, the state or any political division thereof, or for or to any public institution owned or managed and controlled by the state, or any political division thereof.

Section 25. Emergency Governmental Operations; Legislature to Provide for

Notwithstanding any other provision of this constitution, the legislature, in order to insure continuity of state and local governmental operations in periods of emergency caused by enemy attack or by disasters (natural or otherwise), shall have the power and the immediate duty

(1) to provide for prompt and temporary succession to the powers and duties of public offices, of whatever nature and whether filled by election or appointment, the incumbents of which may become unavailable for carrying on the powers and duties of such offices, and

(2) to adopt such other measures as may be necessary and proper for insuring the continuity of governmental operations. Nothing in this article shall be construed to limit in any way the power of the state to deal with emergencies arising from any cause.

ARTICLE IV: EXECUTIVE

Section 1. Executive Power; Election and Terms of Governor and Lieutenant-Governor

The executive power shall be vested in the governor, who shall hold office for four years; the lieutenant-governor shall be chosen at the same time, and for the same term. The governor and lieutenant-governor shall be chosen at the general election held in the year nineteen hundred thirty-eight, and each fourth year thereafter. They shall be chosen jointly, by the casting by each voter of a single vote applicable to both offices, and the legislature by law shall provide for making such choice in such manner. The respective persons having the highest number of votes cast jointly for them for governor and lieutenant-governor respectively shall be elected.

Section 2. Qualifications of Governor and Lieutenant-Governor

No person shall be eligible to the office of governor or lieutenant-governor, except a citizen of the United States, of the age of not less than thirty years, and who shall have been five years next preceding the election a resident of this state.

Section 3. Powers and Duties of Governor; Compensation

The governor shall be commander-in-chief of the military and naval forces of the state. The governor shall have power to convene the legislature, or the senate only, on extraordinary occasions. At extraordinary sessions convened pursuant to the provisions of this section no subject shall be acted upon, except such as the governor may recommend for consideration. The governor shall communicate by message to the legislature at every session the condition of the state, and recommend such matters to it as he or she shall judge expedient. The governor shall expedite all such measures as may be resolved upon by the legislature, and shall take care that the laws are faithfully executed. The governor shall receive for his or her services an annual salary to be fixed by joint resolution of the senate and assembly, and there shall be provided for his or her use a suitable and furnished executive residence.

Section 4. Reprieves, Commutations and Pardons; Powers and Duties of Governor Relating to Grants of

The governor shall have the power to grant reprieves, commutations and pardons after conviction, for all offenses except treason and cases of impeachment, upon such conditions and with such restrictions and limitations, as he or she may think proper, subject to such regulations as may be provided by law relative to the manner of applying for pardons. Upon conviction for treason, the governor shall have power to suspend the execution of the sentence, until the case shall be reported to the legislature at its next meeting, when the legislature shall either pardon, or commute the sentence, direct the execution of the sentence, or grant a further reprieve. The governor shall annually communicate to the legislature each case of reprieve, commutation or pardon granted, stating the name of the convict, the crime of which the convict was convicted, the sentence and its date, and the date of the commutation, pardon or reprieve.

Section 5. When Lieutenant-Governor to Act as Governor

In case of the removal of the governor from office or of his or her death or resignation, the lieutenant-governor shall become governor for the remainder of the term.

In case the governor-elect shall decline to serve or shall die, the lieutenant-governor-elect shall become governor for the full term.

In case the governor is impeached, is absent from the state or is otherwise unable to discharge the powers and duties of the office of governor, the lieutenant-governor shall act as governor until the inability shall cease or until the term of the governor shall expire.

In case of the failure of the governor-elect to take the oath of office at the commencement of his or her term, the lieutenant-governor-elect shall act as governor until the governor shall take the oath.

Section 6. Duties and Compensation of Lieutenant-Governor; Succession to the Governorship

The lieutenant-governor shall possess the same qualifications of eligibility for office as the governor. The lieutenant-governor shall be the president of the senate but shall have only a casting vote therein. The lieutenant- governor shall receive for his or her services an annual salary to be fixed by joint resolution of the senate and assembly.

In case of vacancy in the offices of both governor and lieutenant-governor, a governor and lieutenant-governor shall be elected for the remainder of the term at the next general election happening not less than three months after both offices shall have become vacant. No election of a lieutenant-governor shall be had in any event except at the time of electing a governor.
In case of vacancy in the offices of both governor and lieutenant-governor or if both of them shall be impeached, absent from the state or otherwise unable to discharge the powers and duties of the office of governor, the temporary president of the senate shall act as governor until the inability shall cease or until a governor shall be elected.

In case of vacancy in the office of lieutenant-governor alone, or if the lieutenant-governor shall be impeached, absent from the state or otherwise unable to discharge the duties of office, the temporary president of the senate shall perform all the duties of lieutenant- governor during such vacancy or inability.

If, when the duty of acting as governor devolves upon the temporary president of the senate, there be a vacancy in such office or the temporary president of the senate shall be absent from the state or otherwise unable to discharge the duties of governor, the speaker of the assembly shall act as governor during such vacancy or inability.

The legislature may provide for the devolution of the duty of acting as governor in any case not provided for in this article.

Section 7. Action by Governor on Legislative Bills; Reconsideration after Veto

Every bill which shall have passed the senate and assembly shall, before it becomes a law, be presented to the governor; if the governor approve, he or she shall sign it; but if not, he or she shall return it with his or her objections to the house in which it shall have originated, which shall enter the objections at large on the journal, and proceed to reconsider it. If after such reconsideration, two-thirds of the members elected to that house shall agree to pass the bill, it shall be sent together with the objections, to the other house, by which it shall likewise be reconsidered; and if approved by two-thirds of the members elected to that house, it shall become a law notwithstanding the objections of the governor. In all such cases the votes in both houses shall be determined by yeas and nays, and the names of the members voting shall be entered on the journal of each house respectively. If any bill shall not be returned by the governor within ten days (Sundays excepted) after it shall have been presented to him or her, the same shall be a law in like manner as if he or she had signed it, unless the legislature shall, by their adjournment, prevent its return, in which case it shall not become a law without the approval of the governor. No bill shall become a law after the final adjournment of the legislature, unless approved by the governor within thirty days after such adjournment. If any bill presented to the governor contain several items of appropriation of money, the governor may object to one or more of such items while approving of the other portion of the bill. In such case the governor shall append to the bill, at the time of signing it, a statement of the items to which he or she objects; and the appropriation so objected to shall not take effect. If the legislature be in session, he or she shall transmit to the house in which the bill originated a copy of such statement, and the items objected to shall be separately reconsidered. If on reconsideration one or more of such items be approved by two-thirds of the members elected to each house, the same shall be part of the law, notwithstanding the objections of the governor. All the provisions of this section, in relation to bills not approved by the governor, shall apply in cases in which he or she shall withhold approval from any item or items contained in a bill appropriating money.

Section 8. Departmental Rules and Regulations; Filing; Publication

No rule or regulation made by any state department, board, bureau, officer, authority or commission, except such as relates to the organization or internal management of a state department, board, bureau, authority or commission shall be effective until it is filed in the office of the department of state. The legislature shall provide for the speedy publication of such rules and regulations, by appropriate laws.

ARTICLE V: OFFICERS AND CIVIL DEPARTMENTS

Section 1. Comptroller and Attorney-General; Payment of State Moneys without Audit Void

The comptroller and attorney-general shall be chosen at the same general election as the governor and hold office for the same term, and shall possess the qualifications provided in section 2 of article IV. The legislature shall provide for filling vacancies in the office of comptroller and of attorney-general. No election of a comptroller or an attorney-general shall be had except at the time of electing a governor. The comptroller shall be required:

(1) To audit all vouchers before payment and all official accounts;

(2) to audit the accrual and collection of all revenues and receipts; and

(3) to prescribe such methods of accounting as are necessary for the performance of the foregoing duties. The payment of any money of the state, or of any money under its control, or the refund of any money paid to the state, except upon audit by the comptroller, shall be void, and may be restrained upon the suit of any taxpayer with the consent of the supreme court in appellate division on notice to the attorney-general. In such respect the legislature shall define the powers and duties and may also assign to him or her:

(1) supervision of the accounts of any political subdivision of the state; and

(2) powers and duties pertaining to or connected with the assessment and taxation of real estate, including determination of ratios which the assessed valuation of taxable real property bears to the full valuation thereof, but not including any of those powers and duties reserved to officers of a county, city, town or village by virtue of sections seven and eight of article nine of this constitution. The legislature shall assign to him or her no administrative duties, excepting such as may be incidental to the performance of these functions, any other provision of this constitution to the contrary notwithstanding.

Section 2. Civil Departments in the State Government

There shall be not more than twenty civil departments in the state government, including those referred to in this constitution. The legislature may by law change the names of the departments referred to in this constitution.

Section 3. Assignment of Functions

Subject to the limitations contained in this constitution, the legislature may from time to time assign by law new powers and functions to departments, officers, boards, commissions or executive offices of the governor, and increase, modify or diminish their powers and functions. Nothing contained in this article shall prevent the legislature from creating temporary commissions for special purposes or executive offices of the governor and from reducing the number of departments as provided for in this article, by consolidation or otherwise.

Section 4. Department Heads

The head of the department of audit and control shall be the comptroller and of the department of law, the attorney-general. The head of the department of education shall be The Regents of the University of the State of New York, who shall appoint and at pleasure remove a commissioner of education to be the chief administrative officer of the department. The head of the department of agriculture and markets shall be appointed in a manner to be prescribed by law. Except as otherwise provided in this constitution, the heads of all other departments and the members of all boards and commissions, excepting temporary commissions for special purposes, shall be appointed by the governor by and with the advice and consent of the senate and may be removed by the governor, in a manner to be prescribed by law.

Section 5.

Repealed

Section 6. Civil Service Appointments and Promotions; Veterans' Credits

Appointments and promotions in the civil service of the state and all of the civil divisions thereof, including cities and villages, shall be made according to merit and fitness to be ascertained, as far as practicable, by examination which, as far as practicable, shall be competitive; provided, however, that any member of the armed forces of the United States who served therein in time of war, and who, at the time of such member's appointment or promotion, is a citizen or an alien lawfully admitted for permanent residence in the United States and a resident of this state and is honorably discharged or released under honorable circumstances from such service, shall be entitled to receive five points additional credit in a competitive examination for original appointment and two and one-half points additional credit in an examination for promotion or, if such member was disabled in the actual performance of duty in any war, and his or her disability is certified by the United States department of veterans affairs to be in existence at the time of application for appointment or promotion, he or she shall be entitled to receive ten points additional credit in a competitive examination for original appointment and five points additional credit in an examination for promotion. Such additional credit shall be added to the final earned rating of such member after he or she has qualified in an examination and shall be granted only at the time of establishment of an eligible list. No such member shall receive the additional credit granted by this section after he or she has received one appointment, either original entrance or promotion, from an eligible list on which he or she was allowed the additional credit granted by this section, except where a member has been appointed or promoted from an eligible list on which he or she was allowed additional credit for military service and subsequent to such appointment he or she is disabled as provided in this section, such member shall be entitled to ten points additional credit less the number of points of additional credit allowed for the prior appointment.

Section 7. Membership in Retirement Systems; Benefits Not to Be Diminished nor Impaired

(a) After July first, nineteen hundred forty, membership in any pension or retirement system of the state or of a civil division thereof shall be a contractual relationship, the benefits of which shall not be diminished or impaired.

(b) Notwithstanding subdivision (a) of this section, the public pension of a public officer, as defined in paragraph (c) of this section, who stands convicted of a felony for which such felony has a direct and actual relationship to the performance of the public officer's existing duties, may be reduced or revoked, following notice and a hearing by an appropriate court, as provided by law. The court determination whether to reduce or revoke such pension shall be based on the consideration of factors including the severity of the crime and the proportionality of a reduction or revocation of such pension to such crime. When a court issues an order to reduce or revoke such pension, the court shall consider and determine specific findings as to the amount of such forfeiture, if any, and whether forfeiture, in whole or in part, would result in undue hardship or other inequity upon any dependent children, spouse or other dependents; and other factors as provided by law. The legislature shall enact legislation to implement this amendment taking into account interests of justice.

(c) For the purposes of paragraph (b) of this section, the term "public officer" shall mean:

(i) an official filling an elected office within the state;

(ii) a holder of office filled by direct appointment by the governor of this state, either upon or without senate confirmation;

(iii) a county, city, town or village administrator, manager or equivalent position;

(iv) the head or heads of any state or local government department, division, board, commission, bureau, public benefit corporation, or public authority of this state who are vested with authority, direction and control over such department, division, board, commission, bureau, public benefit corporation or public authority;

(v) the chief fiscal officer or treasurer of any municipal corporation or political subdivision of the state;

(vi) a judge or justice of the unified court system; and

(vii) a legislative, executive, or judicial employee of this state who directly assists in the formulation of legislation, rules, regulations, policy, or judicial decision-making and who is designated as a policymaker as set forth in statute.

(d) Paragraph (b) of this section shall only apply to crimes committed on or after the first of January next succeeding the date upon which the people shall approve and ratify the amendment to the constitution that added this paragraph.

ARTICLE VI: JUDICIARY

Section 1. Unified Court System; Organization; Process

a. There shall be a unified court system for the state. The state-wide courts shall consist of the court of appeals, the supreme court including the appellate divisions thereof, the court of claims, the county court, the surrogate's court and the family court, as hereinafter provided. The legislature shall establish in and for the city of New York, as part of the unified court system for the state, a single, city-wide court of civil jurisdiction and a single, city-wide court of criminal jurisdiction, as hereinafter provided, and may upon the request of the mayor and the local legislative body of the city of New York, merge the two courts into one city-wide court of both civil and criminal jurisdiction. The unified court system for the state shall also include the district, town, city and village courts outside the city of New York, as hereinafter provided.

b. The court of appeals, the supreme court including the appellate divisions thereof, the court of claims, the county court, the surrogate's court, the family court, the courts or court of civil and criminal jurisdiction of the city of New York, and such other courts as the legislature may determine shall be courts of record.
c. All processes, warrants and other mandates of the court of appeals, the supreme court including the appellate divisions thereof, the court of claims, the county court, the surrogate's court and the family court may be served and executed in any part of the state. All processes, warrants and other mandates of the courts or court of civil and criminal jurisdiction of the city of New York may, subject to such limitation as may be prescribed by the legislature, be served and executed in any part of the state. The legislature may provide that processes, warrants and other mandates of the district court may be served and executed in any part of the state and that processes, warrants and other mandates of town, village and city courts outside the city of New York may be served and executed in any part of the county in which such courts are located or in any part of any adjoining

county.

Section 2. Court of Appeals; Organization; Designations; Vacancies, How Filled; Commission on Judicial Nomination

a. The court of appeals is continued. It shall consist of the chief judge and the six elected associate judges now in office, who shall hold their offices until the expiration of their respective terms, and their successors, and such justices of the supreme court as may be designated for service in said court as hereinafter provided. The official terms of the chief judge and the six associate judges shall be fourteen years.

Five members of the court shall constitute a quorum, and the concurrence of four shall be necessary to a decision; but no more than seven judges shall sit in any case. In case of the temporary absence or inability to act of any judge of the court of appeals, the court may designate any justice of the supreme court to serve as associate judge of the court during such absence or inability to act. The court shall have power to appoint and to remove its clerk. The powers and jurisdiction of the court shall not be suspended for want of appointment when the number of judges is sufficient to constitute a quorum.

b. Whenever and as often as the court of appeals shall certify to the governor that the court is unable, by reason of the accumulation of causes pending therein, to hear and dispose of the same with reasonable speed, the governor shall designate such number of justices of the supreme court as may be so certified to be necessary, but not more than four, to serve as associate judges of the court of appeals. The justices so designated shall be relieved, while so serving, from their duties as justices of the supreme court, and shall serve as associate judges of the court of appeals until the court shall certify that the need for the services of any such justices no longer exists, whereupon they shall return to the supreme court. The governor may fill vacancies among such designated judges. No such justices shall serve as associate judge of the court of appeals except while holding the office of justice of the supreme court. The designation of a justice of the supreme court as an associate judge of the court of appeals shall not be deemed to affect his or her existing office any longer than until the expiration of his or her designation as such associate judge, nor to create a vacancy.

c. There shall be a commission on judicial nomination to evaluate the qualifications of candidates for appointment to the court of appeals and to prepare a written report and recommend to the governor those persons who by their character, temperament, professional aptitude and experience are well qualified to hold such judicial office. The legislature shall provide by law for the organization and procedure of the judicial nominating commission.

d. (l) The commission on judicial nomination shall consist of twelve members of whom four shall be appointed by the governor, four by the chief judge of the court of appeals, and one each by the speaker of the assembly, the temporary president of the senate, the minority leader of the senate, and the minority leader of the assembly. Of the four members appointed by the governor, no more than two shall be enrolled in the same political party, two shall be members of the bar of the state, and two shall not be members of the bar of the state. Of the four members appointed by the chief judge of the court of appeals, no more than two shall be enrolled in the same political party, two shall be members of the bar of the state, and two shall not be members of the bar of the state. No member of the commission shall hold or have held any judicial office or hold any elected public office for which he or she receives compensation during his or her period of service, except that the governor and the chief judge may each appoint no more than one former judge or justice of the unified court system to such commission. No member of the commission shall hold any office in any political party. No member of the judicial nominating commission shall be eligible for appointment to judicial office in any court of the state during the member's period of service or within one year thereafter.

(2) The members first appointed by the governor shall have respectively one, two, three and four year terms as the governor shall designate. The members first appointed by the chief judge of the court of appeals shall have respectively one, two, three and four year terms as the chief judge shall designate. The member first appointed by the temporary president of the senate shall have a one-year term. The member first appointed by the minority leader of the senate shall have a two-year term. The member first appointed by the speaker of the assembly shall have a four-year term. The member first appointed by the minority leader of the assembly shall have a three-year term. Each subsequent appointment shall be for a term of four years.

(3) The commission shall designate one of their number to serve as chairperson.

(4) The commission shall consider the qualifications of candidates for appointment to the offices of judge and chief judge of the court of appeals and, whenever a vacancy in those offices occurs, shall prepare a written report and recommend to the governor persons who are well qualified for those judicial offices.

e. The governor shall appoint, with the advice and consent of the senate, from among those recommended by the judicial nominating commission, a person to fill the office of chief judge or associate judge, as the case may be, whenever a vacancy occurs in the court of appeals; provided, however, that no person may be appointed a judge of the court of appeals unless such person is a resident of the state and has been admitted to the practice of law in this state for at least ten years. The governor shall transmit to the senate the written report of the commission on judicial nomination relating to the nominee.

f. When a vacancy occurs in the office of chief judge or associate judge of the court of appeals and the senate is not in session to give its advice and consent to an appointment to fill the vacancy, the governor shall fill the vacancy by interim appointment upon the recommendation of a commission on judicial nomination as provided in this section. An interim appointment shall continue until the senate shall pass upon the governor's selection. If the senate confirms an appointment, the judge shall serve a term as provided in subdivision a of this section commencing from the date of his or her interim appointment. If the senate rejects an appointment, a vacancy in the office shall occur sixty days after such rejection. If an interim appointment to the court of appeals be made from among the justices of the supreme court or the appellate divisions thereof, that appointment shall not affect the justice's existing office, nor create a vacancy in the supreme court, or the appellate division thereof, unless such appointment is confirmed by the senate and the appointee shall assume such office. If an interim appointment of chief judge of the court of appeals be made from among the associate judges, an interim appointment of associate judge shall be made in like manner; in such case, the appointment as chief judge shall not affect the existing office of associate judge, unless such appointment as chief judge is confirmed by the senate and the appointee shall assume such office.

g. The provisions of subdivisions c, d, e and f of this section shall not apply to temporary designations or assignments of judges or justices.

Section 3. Court of Appeals; Jurisdiction

a. The jurisdiction of the court of appeals shall be limited to the review of questions of law except where the judgment is of death, or where the appellate division, on reversing or modifying a final or interlocutory judgment in an action or a final or interlocutory order in a special proceeding, finds new facts and a final judgment or a final order pursuant thereto is entered; but the right to appeal shall not depend upon the amount involved.

b. Appeals to the court of appeals may be taken in the classes of cases hereafter enumerated in this section;

In criminal cases, directly from a court of original jurisdiction where the judgment is of death, and in other criminal cases from an appellate division or otherwise as the legislature may from time to time provide.

In civil cases and proceedings as follows:

(1) As of right, from a judgment or order entered upon the decision of an appellate division of the supreme court which finally determines an action or special proceeding wherein is directly involved the construction of the constitution of the state or of the United States, or where one or more of the justices of the appellate division dissents from the decision of the court, or where the judgment or order is one of reversal or modification.

(2) As of right, from a judgment or order of a court of record of original jurisdiction which finally determines an action or special proceeding where the only question involved on the appeal is the validity of a statutory provision of the state or of the United States under the constitution of the state or of the United States; and on any such appeal only the constitutional question shall be considered and determined by the court.

(3) As of right, from an order of the appellate division granting a new trial in an action or a new hearing in a special proceeding where the appellant stipulates that, upon affirmance, judgment absolute or final order shall be rendered against him or her.

(4) From a determination of the appellate division of the supreme court in any department, other than a judgment or order which finally determines an action or special proceeding, where the appellate division allows the same and certifies that one or more questions of law have arisen which, in its opinion, ought to be reviewed by the court of appeals, but in such case the appeal shall bring up for review only the question or questions so certified; and the court of appeals shall certify to the appellate division its determination upon such question or questions.

(5) From an order of the appellate division of the supreme court in any department, in a proceeding instituted by or against one or more public officers or a board, commission or other body of public officers or a court or tribunal, other than an order which finally determines such proceeding, where the court of appeals shall allow the same upon the ground that, in its opinion, a question of law is involved which ought to be reviewed by it, and without regard to the availability of appeal by stipulation for final order absolute.

(6) From a judgment or order entered upon the decision of an appellate division of the supreme court which finally determines an action or special proceeding but which is not appealable under paragraph (1) of this subdivision where the appellate division or the court of appeals shall certify that in its opinion a question of law is involved which ought to be reviewed by the court of appeals. Such an appeal may be allowed upon application (a) to the appellate division, and in case of refusal, to the court of appeals, or (b) directly to the court of appeals. Such an appeal shall be allowed when required in the interest of substantial justice.

(7) No appeal shall be taken to the court of appeals from a judgment or order entered upon the decision of an appellate division of the supreme court in any civil case or proceeding where the appeal to the appellate division was from a judgment or order entered in an appeal from another court, including an appellate or special term of the supreme court, unless the construction of the constitution of the state or of the United States is directly involved therein, or unless the appellate division of the supreme court shall certify that in its opinion a question of law is involved which ought to be reviewed by the court of appeals.

(8) The legislature may abolish an appeal to the court of appeals as of right in any or all of the cases or classes of cases specified in paragraph (1) of this subdivision wherein no question involving the construction of the constitution of the state or of the United

States is directly involved, provided, however, that appeals in any such case or class of cases shall thereupon be governed by paragraph (6) of this subdivision.

(9) The court of appeals shall adopt and from time to time may amend a rule to permit the court to answer questions of New York law certified to it by the Supreme Court of the United States, a court of appeals of the United States or an appellate court of last resort of another state, which may be determinative of the cause then pending in the certifying court and which in the opinion of the certifying court are not controlled by precedent in the decisions of the courts of New York.

Section 4. Judicial Departments; Appellate Divisions, How Constituted; Governor to Designate Justices; Temporary Assignments; Jurisdiction

a. The state shall be divided into four judicial departments. The first department shall consist of the counties within the first judicial district of the state. The second department shall consist of the counties within the second, ninth, tenth and eleventh judicial districts of the state. The third department shall consist of the counties within the third, fourth and sixth judicial districts of the state. The fourth department shall consist of the counties within the fifth, seventh and eighth judicial districts of the state. Each department shall be bounded by the lines of judicial districts. Once every ten years the legislature may alter the boundaries of the judicial departments, but without changing the number thereof.

b. The appellate divisions of the supreme court are continued, and shall consist of seven justices of the supreme court in each of the first and second departments, and five justices in each of the other departments. In each appellate division, four justices shall constitute a quorum, and the concurrence of three shall be necessary to a decision. No more than five justices shall sit in any case.

c. The governor shall designate the presiding justice of each appellate division, who shall act as such during his or her term of office and shall be a resident of the department. The other justices of the appellate divisions shall be designated by the governor, from all the justices elected to the supreme court, for terms of five years or the unexpired portions of their respective terms of office, if less than five years.

d. The justices heretofore designated shall continue to sit in the appellate divisions until the terms of their respective designations shall expire. From time to time as the terms of the designations expire, or vacancies occur, the governor shall make new designations. The governor may also, on request of any appellate division, make temporary designations in case of the absence or inability to act of any justice in such appellate division, for service only during such absence or inability to act.

e. In case any appellate division shall certify to the governor that one or more additional justices are needed for the speedy disposition of the business before it, the governor may designate an additional justice or additional justices; but when the need for such additional justice or justices shall no longer exist, the appellate division shall so certify to the governor, and thereupon service under such designation or designations shall cease.

f. A majority of the justices designated to sit in any appellate division shall at all times be residents of the department.

g. Whenever the appellate division in any department shall be unable to dispose of its business within a reasonable time, a majority of the presiding justices of the several departments, at a meeting called by the presiding justice of the department in arrears, may transfer any pending appeals from such department to any other department for hearing and determination.

h. A justice of the appellate division of the supreme court in any department may be temporarily designated by the presiding justice of his or her department to the appellate division in another judicial department upon agreement by the presiding justices of the appellate division of the departments concerned.

i. In the event that the disqualification, absence or inability to act of justices in any appellate division prevents there being a quorum of justices qualified to hear an appeal, the justices qualified to hear the appeal may transfer it to the appellate division in another department for hearing and determination. In the event that the justices in any appellate division qualified to hear an appeal are equally divided, said justices may transfer the appeal to the appellate division in another department for hearing and determination. Each appellate division shall have power to appoint and remove its clerk.

j. No justice of the appellate division shall, within the department to which he or she may be designated to perform the duties of an appellate justice, exercise any of the powers of a justice of the supreme court, other than those of a justice out of court, and those pertaining to the appellate division, except that the justice may decide causes or proceedings theretofore submitted, or hear and decide motions submitted by consent of counsel, but any such justice, when not actually engaged in performing the duties of such appellate justice in the department to which he or she is designated, may hold any term of the supreme court and exercise any of the powers of a justice of the supreme court in any judicial district in any other department of the state.

k. The appellate divisions of the supreme court shall have all the jurisdiction possessed by them on the effective date of this article and such additional jurisdiction as may be prescribed by law, provided, however, that the right to appeal to the appellate divisions from a judgment or order which does not finally determine an action or special proceeding may be limited or conditioned by law.

Section 5. Appeals from Judgment or Order; New Trial

a. Upon an appeal from a judgment or an order, any appellate court to which the appeal is taken which is authorized to review such judgment or order may reverse or affirm, wholly or in part, or may modify the judgment or order appealed from, and each interlocutory judgment or intermediate or other order which it is authorized to review, and as to any or all of the parties. It shall thereupon render judgment of affirmance, judgment of reversal and final judgment upon the right of any or all of the parties, or judgment of modification thereon according to law, except where it may be necessary or proper to grant a new trial or hearing, when it may grant a new trial or hearing.

b. If any appeal is taken to an appellate court which is not authorized to review such judgment or order, the court shall transfer the appeal to an appellate court which is authorized to review such judgment or order.

Section 6. Judicial Districts; How Constituted; Supreme Court

a. The state shall be divided into eleven judicial districts. The first judicial district shall consist of the counties of Bronx and New York. The second judicial district shall consist of the counties of Kings and Richmond. The third judicial district shall consist of the counties of Albany, Columbia, Greene, Rensselaer, Schoharie, Sullivan, and Ulster. The fourth judicial district shall consist of the counties of Clinton, Essex, Franklin, Fulton, Hamilton, Montgomery, St. Lawrence, Saratoga, Schenectady, Warren and Washington. The fifth judicial district shall consist of the counties of Herkimer, Jefferson, Lewis, Oneida, Onondaga, and Oswego. The sixth judicial district shall consist of the counties of Broome, Chemung, Chenango, Cortland, Delaware, Madison, Otsego, Schuyler, Tioga and Tompkins. The seventh judicial district shall consist of the counties of Cayuga, Livingston, Monroe, Ontario, Seneca, Steuben, Wayne and Yates. The eighth judicial district shall consist of the counties of Allegany, Cattaraugus, Chautauqua, Erie, Genesee, Niagara, Orleans and

Wyoming. The ninth judicial district shall consist of the counties of Dutchess, Orange, Putnam, Rockland and Westchester. The tenth judicial district shall consist of the counties of Nassau and Suffolk. The eleventh judicial district shall consist of the county of Queens.

b. Once every ten years the legislature may increase or decrease the number of judicial districts or alter the composition of judicial districts and thereupon re-apportion the justices to be thereafter elected in the judicial districts so altered. Each judicial district shall be bounded by county lines.

c. The justices of the supreme court shall be chosen by the electors of the judicial district in which they are to serve. The terms of justices of the supreme court shall be fourteen years from and including the first day of January next after their election.

d. The supreme court is continued. It shall consist of the number of justices of the supreme court including the justices designated to the appellate divisions of the supreme court, judges of the county court of the counties of Bronx, Kings, Queens and Richmond and judges of the court of general sessions of the county of New York authorized by law on the thirty-first day of August next after the approval and ratification of this amendment by the people, all of whom shall be justices of the supreme court for the remainder of their terms. The legislature may increase the number of justices of the supreme court in any judicial district, except that the number in any district shall not be increased to exceed one justice for fifty thousand, or fraction over thirty thousand, of the population thereof as shown by the last federal census or state enumeration. The legislature may decrease the number of justices of the supreme court in any judicial district, except that the number in any district shall not be less than the number of justices of the supreme court authorized by law on the effective date of this article.

e. The clerks of the several counties shall be clerks of the supreme court, with such powers and duties as shall be prescribed by law.

Section 7. Supreme Court; Jurisdiction

a. The supreme court shall have general original jurisdiction in law and equity and the appellate jurisdiction herein provided. In the city of New York, it shall have exclusive jurisdiction over crimes prosecuted by indictment, provided, however, that the legislature may grant to the city-wide court of criminal jurisdiction of the city of New York jurisdiction over misdemeanors prosecuted by indictment and to the family court in the city of New York jurisdiction over crimes and offenses by or against minors or between spouses or between parent and child or between members of the same family or household.

b. If the legislature shall create new classes of actions and proceedings, the supreme court shall have jurisdiction over such classes of actions and proceedings, but the legislature may provide that another court or other courts shall also have jurisdiction and that actions and proceedings of such classes may be originated in such other court or courts.

Section 8. Appellate Terms; Composition; Jurisdiction

a. The appellate division of the supreme court in each judicial department may establish an appellate term in and for such department or in and for a judicial district or districts or in and for a county or counties within such department. Such an appellate term shall be composed of not less than three nor more than five justices of the supreme court who shall be designated from time to time by the chief administrator of the courts with the approval of the presiding justice of the appropriate appellate division, and who shall be residents of the department or of the judicial district or districts as the case may be and the chief administrator of the courts shall designate the place or places where such appellate terms shall be held.

b. Any such appellate term may be discontinued and re-established as the appellate division of the supreme court in each department shall determine from time to time and any designation to service therein may be revoked by the chief administrator of the courts with the approval of the presiding justice of the appropriate appellate division.

c. In each appellate term no more than three justices assigned thereto shall sit in any action or proceeding. Two of such justices shall constitute a quorum and the concurrence of two shall be necessary to a decision.

d. If so directed by the appellate division of the supreme court establishing an appellate term, an appellate term shall have jurisdiction to hear and determine appeals now or hereafter authorized by law to be taken to the supreme court or to the appellate division other than appeals from the supreme court, a surrogate's court, the family court or appeals in criminal cases prosecuted by indictment or by information as provided in section six of article one.

e. As may be provided by law, an appellate term shall have jurisdiction to hear and determine appeals from the district court or a town, village or city court outside the city of New York.

Section 9. Court of Claims; Jurisdiction

The court of claims is continued. It shall consist of the eight judges now authorized by law, but the legislature may increase such number and may reduce such number to six or seven. The judges shall be appointed by the governor by and with the advice and consent of the senate and their terms of office shall be nine years. The court shall have jurisdiction to hear and determine claims against the state or by the state against the claimant or between conflicting claimants as the legislature may provide.

Section 10. County Courts; Judges

a. The county court is continued in each county outside the city of New York. There shall be at least one judge of the county court in each county and such number of additional judges in each county as may be provided by law. The judges shall be residents of the county and shall be chosen by the electors of the county.

b. The terms of the judges of the county court shall be ten years from and including the first day of January next after their election.

Section 11. County Court; Jurisdiction

a. The county court shall have jurisdiction over the following classes of actions and proceedings which shall be originated in such county court in the manner provided by law, except that actions and proceedings within the jurisdiction of the district court or a town, village or city court outside the city of New York may, as provided by law, be originated therein: actions and proceedings for the recovery of money, actions and proceedings for the recovery of chattels and actions and proceedings for the foreclosure of mechanics liens and liens on personal property where the amount sought to be recovered or the value of the property does not exceed twenty-five thousand dollars exclusive of interest and costs; over all crimes and other violations of law; over summary proceedings to recover possession of real property and to remove tenants therefrom; and over such other actions and proceedings, not within the exclusive jurisdiction of the supreme court, as may be provided by law.

b. The county court shall exercise such equity jurisdiction as may be provided by law and its jurisdiction to enter judgment upon a counterclaim for the recovery of money only shall be unlimited.

c. The county court shall have jurisdiction to hear and determine all appeals arising in the county in the following actions and proceedings: as of right, from a judgment or order of the district court or a town, village or city court which finally determines an action or proceeding and, as may be provided by law, from a judgment or order of any such court which does not finally determine an action or proceeding. The legislature may provide, in accordance with the provisions of section eight of this article, that any or all of such appeals be taken to an appellate term of the supreme court instead of the county court.

d. The provisions of this section shall in no way limit or impair the jurisdiction of the supreme court as set forth in section seven of this article.

Section 12. Surrogate's Courts; Judges; Jurisdiction

a. The surrogate's court is continued in each county in the state. There shall be at least one judge of the surrogate's court in each county and such number of additional judges of the surrogate's court as may be provided by law.

b. The judges of the surrogate's court shall be residents of the county and shall be chosen by the electors of the county.

c. The terms of the judges of the surrogate's court in the city of New York shall be fourteen years, and in other counties ten years, from and including the first day of January next after their election.

d. The surrogate's court shall have jurisdiction over all actions and proceedings relating to the affairs of decedents, probate of wills, administration of estates and actions and proceedings arising thereunder or pertaining thereto, guardianship of the property of minors, and such other actions and proceedings, not within the exclusive jurisdiction of the supreme court, as may be provided by law.

e. The surrogate's court shall exercise such equity jurisdiction as may be provided by law.

f. The provisions of this section shall in no way limit or impair the jurisdiction of the supreme court as set forth in section seven of this article.

Section 13. Family Court; Organization; Jurisdiction

a. The family court of the state of New York is hereby established. It shall consist of at least one judge in each county outside the city of New York and such number of additional judges for such counties as may be provided by law. Within the city of New York it shall consist of such number of judges as may be provided by law. The judges of the family court within the city of New York shall be residents of such city and shall be appointed by the mayor of the city of New York for terms of ten years. The judges of the family court outside the city of New York, shall be chosen by the electors of the counties wherein they reside for terms of ten years.

b. The family court shall have jurisdiction over the following classes of actions and proceedings which shall be originated in such family court in the manner provided by law: (1) the protection, treatment, correction and commitment of those minors who are in need of the exercise of the authority of the court because of circumstances of neglect, delinquency or dependency, as the legislature may determine; (2) the custody of minors except for custody incidental to actions and proceedings for marital separation, divorce, annulment of marriage and dissolution of marriage; (3) the adoption of persons; (4) the support of dependents except for support incidental to actions and proceedings in this state for marital separation, divorce, annulment of marriage or dissolution of marriage; (5) the establishment of paternity; (6) proceedings for conciliation of spouses; and (7) as may be provided by law: the guardianship of the person of minors and, in conformity with the provisions of section seven of this article, crimes and offenses by or against minors or between spouses or between parent and child or between members of the same family or household. Nothing in this section shall be construed to abridge the authority or jurisdiction of courts to appoint guardians in cases originating in those courts.

c. The family court shall also have jurisdiction to determine, with the same powers possessed by the supreme court, the following matters when referred to the family court from the supreme court: habeas corpus proceedings for the determination of the custody of minors; and in actions and proceedings for marital separation, divorce, annulment of marriage and dissolution of marriage, applications to fix temporary or permanent support and custody, or applications to enforce judgments and orders of support and of custody, or applications to modify judgments and orders of support and of custody which may be granted only upon the showing to the family court that there has been a subsequent change of circumstances and that modification is required.

d. The provisions of this section shall in no way limit or impair the jurisdiction of the supreme court as set forth in section seven of this article.

Section 14. Discharge of Duties of More Than One Judicial Office by Same Judicial Officer

The legislature may at any time provide that outside the city of New York the same person may act and discharge the duties of county judge and surrogate or of judge of the family court and surrogate, or of county judge and judge of the family court, or of all three positions in any county.

Section 15. New York City; City-Wide Courts; Jurisdiction

a. The legislature shall by law establish a single court of city-wide civil jurisdiction and a single court of city-wide criminal jurisdiction in and for the city of New York and the legislature may, upon the request of the mayor and the local legislative body of the city of New York, merge the two courts into one city-wide court of both civil and criminal jurisdiction. The said city-wide courts shall consist of such number of judges as may be provided by law. The judges of the court of city-wide civil jurisdiction shall be residents of such city and shall be chosen for terms of ten years by the electors of the counties included within the city of New York from districts within such counties established by law. The judges of the court of city-wide criminal jurisdiction shall be residents of such city and shall be appointed for terms of ten years by the mayor of the city of New York.

b. The court of city-wide civil jurisdiction of the city of New York shall have jurisdiction over the following classes of actions and proceedings which shall be originated in such court in the manner provided by law: actions and proceedings for the recovery of money, actions and proceedings for the recovery of chattels and actions and proceedings for the foreclosure of mechanics liens and liens on personal property where the amount sought to be recovered or the value of the property does not exceed twenty-five thousand dollars exclusive of interest and costs, or such smaller amount as may be fixed by law; over summary proceedings to recover possession of real property and to remove tenants therefrom and over such other actions and proceedings, not within the exclusive jurisdiction of the supreme court, as may be provided by law. The court of city-wide civil jurisdiction shall further exercise such equity jurisdiction as may be provided by law and its jurisdiction to enter judgment upon a counterclaim for the recovery of money only shall be unlimited.

c. The court of city-wide criminal jurisdiction of the city of New York shall have jurisdiction over crimes and other violations of law, other than those prosecuted by indictment, provided, however, that the legislature may grant to said court jurisdiction over misdemeanors prosecuted by indictment; and over such other actions and proceedings, not within the exclusive jurisdiction of the supreme court, as may be provided by law.

d. The provisions of this section shall in no way limit or impair the jurisdiction of the supreme court as set forth in section seven of this article.

Section 16. District Courts; Jurisdiction; Judges

a. The district court of Nassau county may be continued under existing law and the legislature may, at the request of the board of supervisors or other elective governing body of any county outside the city of New York, establish the district court for the entire area of such county or for a portion of such county consisting of one or more cities, or one or more towns which are contiguous, or of a combination of such cities and such towns provided at least one of such cities is contiguous to one of such towns.

b. No law establishing the district court for an entire county shall become effective unless approved at a general election on the question of the approval of such law by a majority of the votes cast thereon by the electors within the area of any cities in the county considered as one unit and by a majority of the votes cast thereon by the electors within the area outside of cities in the county considered as one unit. c. No law establishing the district court for a portion of a county shall become effective unless approved at a general election on the question of the approval of such law by a majority of the votes cast thereon by the electors within the area of any cities included in such portion of the county considered as one unit and by a majority of the votes cast thereon by the electors within the area outside of cities included in such portion of the county considered as one unit.

d. The district court shall have such jurisdiction as may be provided by law, but not in any respect greater than the jurisdiction of the courts for the city of New York as provided in section fifteen of this article, provided, however, that in actions and proceedings for the recovery of money, actions and proceedings for the recovery of chattels and actions and proceedings for the foreclosure of mechanics liens and liens on personal property, the amount sought to be recovered or the value of the property shall not exceed fifteen thousand dollars exclusive of interest and costs.

e. The legislature may create districts of the district court which shall consist of an entire county or of an area less than a county.

f. There shall be at least one judge of the district court for each district and such number of additional judges in each district as may be provided by law.

g. The judges of the district court shall be apportioned among the districts as may be provided by law, and to the extent practicable, in accordance with the population and the volume of judicial business.

h. The judges shall be residents of the district and shall be chosen by the electors of the district. Their terms shall be six years from and including the first day of January next after their election.

i. The legislature may regulate and discontinue the district court in any county or portion thereof.

Section 17. Town, Village and City Courts; Jurisdiction; Judges

a. Courts for towns, villages and cities outside the city of New York are continued and shall have the jurisdiction prescribed by the legislature but not in any respect greater than the jurisdiction of the district court as provided in section sixteen of this article.

b. The legislature may regulate such courts, establish uniform jurisdiction, practice and procedure for city courts outside the city of New York and may discontinue any village or city court outside the city of New York existing on the effective date of this article. The legislature may discontinue any town court existing on the effective date of this article only with the approval of a majority of the total votes cast at a general election on the question of a proposed discontinuance of the court in each such town affected thereby.

c. The legislature may abolish the legislative functions on town boards of justices of the peace and provide that town councilmen be elected in their stead.

d. The number of the judges of each of such town, village and city courts and the classification and duties of the judges shall be prescribed by the legislature. The terms, method of selection and method of filling vacancies for the judges of such courts shall be prescribed by the legislature, provided, however, that the justices of town courts shall be chosen by the electors of the town for terms of four years from and including the first day of January next after their election.

Section 18. Trial by Jury; Trial without Jury; Claims Against State

a. Trial by jury is guaranteed as provided in article one of this constitution. The legislature may provide that in any court of original jurisdiction a jury shall be composed of six or of twelve persons and may authorize any court which shall have jurisdiction over crimes and other violations of law, other than crimes prosecuted by indictment, to try such matters without a jury, provided, however, that crimes prosecuted by indictment shall be tried by a jury composed of twelve persons, unless a jury trial has been waived as provided in section two of article one of this constitution.

b. The legislature may provide for the manner of trial of actions and proceedings involving claims against the state.

Section 19. Transfer of Actions and Proceedings

a. The supreme court may transfer any action or proceeding, except one over which it shall have exclusive jurisdiction which does not depend upon the monetary amount sought, to any other court having jurisdiction of the subject matter within the judicial department provided that such other court has jurisdiction over the classes of persons named as parties. As may be provided by law, the supreme court may transfer to itself any action or proceeding originated or pending in another court within the judicial department other than the court of claims upon a finding that such a transfer will promote the administration of justice.

b. The county court shall transfer to the supreme court or surrogate's court or family court any action or proceeding which has not been transferred to it from the supreme court or surrogate's court or family court and over which the county court has no jurisdiction. The county court may transfer any action or proceeding, except a criminal action or proceeding involving a felony prosecuted by indictment or an action or proceeding required by this article to be dealt with in the surrogate's court or family court, to any court, other than the supreme court, having jurisdiction of the subject matter within the county provided that such other court has jurisdiction over the classes of persons named as parties.

c. As may be provided by law, the supreme court or the county court may transfer to the county court any action or proceeding originated or pending in the district court or a town, village or city court outside the city of New York upon a finding that such a transfer will promote the administration of justice.

d. The surrogate's court shall transfer to the supreme court or the county court or the family court or the courts for the city of New York established pursuant to section fifteen of this article any action or proceeding which has not been transferred to it from any of said courts and over which the surrogate's court has no jurisdiction.

e. The family court shall transfer to the supreme court or the surrogate's court or the county court or the courts for the city of New York established pursuant to section fifteen of this article any action or proceeding which has not been transferred to it from any of said courts and over which the family court has no jurisdiction.

f. The courts for the city of New York established pursuant to section fifteen of this article shall transfer to the supreme court or the surrogate's court or the family court any action or proceeding which has not been transferred to them from any of said courts and over which the said courts for the city of New York have no jurisdiction.

g. As may be provided by law, the supreme court shall transfer any action or proceeding to any other court having jurisdiction of the subject matter in any other judicial district or county provided that such other court has jurisdiction over the classes of persons named as parties.

h. As may be provided by law, the county court, the surrogate's court, the family court and the courts for the city of New York established pursuant to section fifteen of this article may transfer any action or proceeding, other than one which has previously been transferred to it, to any other court, except the supreme court, having jurisdiction of the subject matter in any other judicial district or county provided that such other court has jurisdiction over the classes of persons named as parties.

i. As may be provided by law, the district court or a town, village or city court outside the city of New York may transfer any action or proceeding, other than one which has previously been transferred to it, to any court, other than the county court or the surrogate's court or the family court or the supreme court, having jurisdiction of the subject matter in the same or an adjoining county provided that such other court has jurisdiction over the classes of persons named as parties.

j. Each court shall exercise jurisdiction over any action or proceeding transferred to it pursuant to this section.

k. The legislature may provide that the verdict or judgment in actions and proceedings so transferred shall not be subject to the limitation of monetary jurisdiction of the court to which the actions and proceedings are transferred if that limitation be lower than that of the court in which the actions and proceedings were originated.

Section 20. Judges and Justices; Qualifications; Eligibility for Other Office or Service; Restrictions

a. No person, other than one who holds such office at the effective date of this article, may assume the office of judge of the court of appeals, justice of the supreme court, or judge of the court of claims unless he or she has been admitted to practice law in this state at least ten years. No person, other than one who holds such office at the effective date of this article, may assume the office of judge of the county court, surrogate's court, family court, a court for the city of New York established pursuant to section fifteen of this article, district court or city court outside the city of New York unless he or she has been admitted to practice law in this state at least five years or such greater number of years as the legislature may determine.

b. A judge of the court of appeals, justice of the supreme court, judge of the court of claims, judge of a county court, judge of the surrogate's court, judge of the family court or judge of a court for the city of New York established pursuant to section fifteen of this article who is elected or appointed after the effective date of this article may not:

(1) hold any other public office or trust except an office in relation to the administration of the courts, member of a constitutional convention or member of the armed forces of the United States or of the state of New York in which latter event the legislature may enact such legislation as it deems appropriate to provide for a temporary judge or justice to serve during the period of the absence of such judge or justice in the armed forces;

(2) be eligible to be a candidate for any public office other than judicial office or member of a constitutional convention, unless he or she resigns from judicial office; in the event a judge or justice does not so resign from judicial office within ten days after his or her acceptance of the nomination of such other office, his or her judicial office shall become vacant and the vacancy shall be filled in the manner provided in this article;

(3) hold any office or assume the duties or exercise the powers of any office of any political organization or be a member of any governing or executive agency thereof;

(4) engage in the practice of law, act as an arbitrator, referee or compensated mediator in any action or proceeding or matter or engage in the conduct of any other profession or business which interferes with the performance of his or her judicial duties. Judges and justices of the courts specified in this subdivision shall also be subject to such rules of conduct as may be promulgated by the chief administrator of the courts with the approval of the court of appeals.

c. Qualifications for and restrictions upon the judges of district, town, village or city courts outside the city of New York, other than such qualifications and restrictions specifically set forth in subdivision a of this section, shall be prescribed by the legislature, provided, however, that the legislature shall require a course of training and education to be completed by justices of town and village courts selected after the effective date of this article who have not been admitted to practice law in this state. Judges of such courts shall also be subject to such rules of conduct not inconsistent with laws as may be promulgated by the chief administrator of the courts with the approval of the court of appeals.

Section 21. Vacancies; How Filled

a. When a vacancy shall occur, otherwise than by expiration of term, in the office of justice of the supreme court, of judge of the county court, of judge of the surrogate's court or judge of the family court outside the city of New York, it shall be filled for a full term at the next general election held not less than three months after such vacancy occurs and until the vacancy shall be so filled, the governor by and with the advice and consent of the senate, if the senate shall be in session, or, if the senate not be in session, the governor may fill such vacancy by an appointment which shall continue until and including the last day of December next after the election at which the vacancy shall be filled.

b. When a vacancy shall occur, otherwise than by expiration of term, in the office of judge of the court of claims, it shall be filled for the unexpired term in the same manner as an original appointment.

c. When a vacancy shall occur, otherwise than by expiration of term, in the office of judge elected to the city-wide court of civil jurisdiction of the city of New York, it shall be filled for a full term at the next general election held not less than three months after such vacancy occurs and, until the vacancy shall be so filled, the mayor of the city of New York may fill such vacancy by an appointment which shall continue until and including the last day of December next after the election at which the vacancy shall be filled. When a vacancy shall occur, otherwise than by expiration of term on the last day of December of any year, in the office of judge appointed to the family court within the city of New York or the city-wide court of criminal jurisdiction of the city of New York, the mayor of the city of New York shall fill such vacancy by an appointment for the unexpired term.

d. When a vacancy shall occur, otherwise than by expiration of term, in the office of judge of the district court, it shall be filled for a full term at the next general election held not less than three months after such vacancy occurs and, until the vacancy shall be so filled, the board of supervisors or the supervisor or supervisors of the affected district if such district consists of a portion of a county or, in counties with an elected county executive officer, such county executive officer may, subject to confirmation by the board of supervisors or the supervisor or supervisors of such district, fill such vacancy by an appointment which shall continue until and including the last day of December next after the election at which the vacancy shall be filled.

Section 22. Commission on Judicial Conduct; Composition; Organization and Procedure; Review by Court of Appeals; Discipline of Judges or Justices

a. There shall be a commission on judicial conduct. The commission on judicial conduct shall receive, initiate, investigate and hear complaints with respect to the conduct, qualifications, fitness to perform or performance of official duties of any judge or justice of the unified court system, in the manner provided by law; and, in accordance with subdivision d of this section, may determine that a judge or justice be admonished, censured or removed from office for cause, including, but not limited to, misconduct in office, persistent failure to perform his or her duties, habitual intemperance, and conduct, on or off the bench, prejudicial to the administration of justice, or that a judge or justice be retired for mental or physical disability preventing the proper performance of his or her judicial duties. The commission shall transmit an (7) such determination to the chief judge of the court of appeals who shall cause written notice of such determination to be given to the judge or justice involved. Such judge or justice may either accept the commission's determination or make written request to the chief judge, within thirty days after receipt of such notice, for a review of such determination by the court of appeals.

b. (I) The commission on judicial conduct shall consist of eleven members, of whom four shall be appointed by the governor, one by the temporary president of the senate, one by the minority leader of the senate, one by the speaker of the assembly, one by the minority leader of the assembly and three by the chief judge of the court of appeals. Of the members appointed by the governor one person shall be a member of the bar of the state but not a judge or justice, two shall not be members of the bar, justices or judges or retired justices or judges of the unified court system, and one shall be a judge or justice of the unified court system. Of the members appointed by the chief judge one person shall be a justice of the appellate division of the supreme court and two shall be judges or justices of a court or courts other than the court of appeals or appellate divisions. None of the persons to be appointed by the legislative leaders shall be justices or judges or retired justices or judges.

(2) The persons first appointed by the governor shall have respectively one, two, three, and four-year terms as the governor shall designate. The persons first appointed by the chief judge of the court of appeals shall have respectively two, three, and four-year terms as the governor shall designate. The person first appointed by the temporary president of the senate shall have a one-year term. The person first appointed by the minority leader of the senate shall have a two-year term. The person first appointed by the speaker of the assembly shall have a four-year term. The person first appointed by the minority leader of the assembly shall have a three-year term. Each member of the commission shall be appointed thereafter for a term of four years. Commission membership of a judge or justice appointed by the governor or the chief judge shall terminate if such member ceases to hold the judicial position which qualified him or her for such appointment. Membership shall also terminate if a member attains a position which would have rendered him or her ineligible for appointment at the time of appointment. A vacancy shall be filled by the appointing officer for the remainder of the term.

c. The organization and procedure of the commission on judicial conduct shall be as provided by law. The commission on judicial conduct may establish its own rules and procedures not inconsistent with law. Unless the legislature shall provide otherwise, the commission shall be empowered to designate one of its members or any other person as a referee to hear and report concerning any matter before the commission.

d. In reviewing a determination of the commission on judicial conduct, the court of appeals may admonish, censure, remove or retire, for the reasons set forth in subdivision a of this section, any judge of the unified court system. In reviewing a determination of the commission on judicial conduct, the court of appeals shall review the commission's findings of fact and conclusions of law on the record of the proceedings upon which the commission's determination was based. The court of appeals may impose a less or more severe sanction prescribed by this section than the one determined by the commission, or impose no sanction.

e. The court of appeals may suspend a judge or justice from exercising the powers of his or her office while there is pending a determination by the commission on judicial conduct for his or her removal or retirement, or while the judge or justice is charged in this state with a felony by an indictment or an information filed pursuant to section six of article one. The suspension shall continue upon conviction and, if the conviction becomes final, the judge or justice shall be removed from office. The suspension shall be terminated upon reversal of the conviction and dismissal of the accusatory instrument. Nothing in this subdivision shall prevent the commission on judicial conduct from determining that a judge or justice be admonished, censured, removed, or retired pursuant to subdivision a of this section.

f. Upon the recommendation of the commission on judicial conduct or on its own motion, the court of appeals may suspend a judge or justice from office when he or she is charged with a crime punishable as a felony under the laws of this state, or any other crime which involves moral turpitude. The suspension shall continue upon conviction and, if the conviction becomes final, the judge or justice shall be removed from office. The suspension shall be terminated upon reversal of the conviction and dismissal of the accusatory instrument. Nothing in this subdivision shall prevent the commission on judicial conduct from determining that a judge or justice be admonished, censured, removed, or retired pursuant to subdivision a of this section.

g. A judge or justice who is suspended from office by the court of appeals shall receive his or her judicial salary during such period of suspension, unless the court directs otherwise. If the court has so directed and such suspension is thereafter terminated, the court may direct that the judge or justice shall be paid his or her salary for such period of suspension.

h. A judge or justice retired by the court of appeals shall be considered to have retired voluntarily. A judge or justice removed by the court of appeals shall be ineligible to hold other judicial office.

i. Notwithstanding any other provision of this section, the legislature may provide by law for review of determinations of the commission on judicial conduct with respect to justices of town and village courts by an appellate division of the supreme court. In such event, all references in this section to the court of appeals and the chief judge thereof shall be deemed references to an appellate division and the presiding justice thereof, respectively.

j. If a court on the judiciary shall have been convened before the effective date of this section and the proceeding shall not be concluded by that date, the court on the judiciary shall have continuing jurisdiction beyond the effective date of this section to conclude the proceeding. All matters pending before the former commission on judicial conduct on the effective date of this section shall be disposed of in such manner as shall be provided by law.

Section 23. Removal of Judges

a. Judges of the court of appeals and justices of the supreme court may be removed by concurrent resolution of both houses of the legislature, if two-thirds of all the members elected to each house concur therein.

b. Judges of the court of claims, the county court, the surrogate's court, the family court, the courts for the city of New York established pursuant to section fifteen of this article, the district court and such other courts as the legislature may determine may be removed by the senate, on the recommendation of the governor, if two-thirds of all the members elected to the senate concur therein.

c. No judge or justice shall be removed by virtue of this section except for cause, which shall be entered on the journals, nor unless he or she shall have been served with a statement of the cause alleged, and shall have had an opportunity to be heard. On the question of removal, the yeas and nays shall be entered on the journal.

Section 24. Court for Trial of Impeachments; Judgment

The assembly shall have the power of impeachment by a vote of a majority of all the members elected thereto. The court for the trial of impeachments shall be composed of the president of the senate, the senators, or the major part of them, and the judges of the court of appeals, or the major part of them. On the trial of an impeachment against the governor or lieutenant-governor, neither the lieutenant- governor nor the temporary president of the senate shall act as a member of the court. No judicial officer shall exercise his or her office after articles of impeachment against him or her shall have been preferred to the senate, until he or she shall have been acquitted. Before the trial of an impeachment, the members of the court shall take an oath or affirmation truly and impartially to try the impeachment according to the evidence, and no person shall be convicted without the concurrence of two-thirds of the members present. Judgment in cases of impeachment shall not extend further than to removal from office, or removal from office and disqualification to hold and enjoy any public office of honor, trust, or profit under this state; but the party impeached shall be liable to indictment and punishment according to law.

Section 25. Judges and Justices; Compensation; Retirement

a. The compensation of a judge of the court of appeals, a justice of the supreme court, a judge of the court of claims, a judge of the county court, a judge of the surrogate's court, a judge of the family court, a judge of a court for the city of New York established pursuant to section fifteen of this article, a judge of the district court or of a retired judge or justice shall be established by law and shall not be diminished during the term of office for which he or she was elected or appointed. Any judge or justice of a court abolished by section thirty-five of this article, who pursuant to that section becomes a judge or justice of a court established or continued by this article, shall receive without interruption or diminution for the remainder of the term for which he or she was elected or appointed to the abolished court the compensation he or she had been receiving upon the effective date of this article together with any additional compensation that may be prescribed by law.

b. Each judge of the court of appeals, justice of the supreme court, judge of the court of claims, judge of the county court, judge of the surrogate's court, judge of the family court, judge of a court for the city of New York established pursuant to section fifteen of this article and judge of the district court shall retire on the last day of December in the year in which he or she reaches the age of seventy. Each such former judge of the court of appeals and justice of the supreme court may thereafter perform the duties of a justice of the supreme court, with power to hear and determine actions and proceedings, provided, however, that it shall be certificated in the manner provided by law that the services of such judge or justice are necessary to expedite the business of the court and that he or she is mentally and physically able and competent to perform the full duties of such office. Any such certification shall be valid for a term of two years and may be extended as provided by law for additional terms of two years. A retired judge or justice shall serve no longer than until the last day of December in the year in which he or she reaches the age of seventy-six. A retired judge or justice shall be subject to assignment by the appellate division of the supreme court of the judicial department of his or her residence. Any retired justice of the supreme court who had been designated to and served as a justice of any appellate division immediately preceding his or her reaching the age of seventy shall be eligible for designation by the governor as a temporary or additional justice of the appellate division. A retired judge or justice shall not be counted in determining the number of justices in a judicial district for purposes of subdivision d of section six of this article.

c. The provisions of this section shall also be applicable to any judge or justice who has not reached the age of seventy-six and to whom it would otherwise have been applicable but for the fact that he or she reached the age of seventy and retired before the effective date of this article.

Section 26. Temporary Assignments of Judges and Justices

a. A justice of the supreme court may perform the duties of office or hold court in any county and may be temporarily assigned to the supreme court in any judicial district or to the court of claims. A justice of the supreme court in the city of New York may be temporarily assigned to the family court in the city of New York or to the surrogate's court in any county within the city of New York when required to dispose of the business of such court.

b. A judge of the court of claims may perform the duties of office or hold court in any county and may be temporarily assigned to the supreme court in any judicial district.

c. A judge of the county court may perform the duties of office or hold court in any county and may be temporarily assigned to the supreme court in the judicial department of his or her residence or to the county court or the family court in any county or to the surrogate's court in any county outside the city of New York or to a court for the city of New York established pursuant to section fifteen of this article.

d. A judge of the surrogate's court in any county within the city of New York may perform the duties of office or hold court in any county and may be temporarily assigned to the supreme court in the judicial department of his or her residence.

e. A judge of the surrogate's court in any county outside the city of New York may perform the duties of office or hold court in any county and may be temporarily assigned to the supreme court in the judicial department of his or her residence or to the county court or the family court in any county or to a court for the city of New York established pursuant to section fifteen of this article.

f. A judge of the family court may perform the duties of office or hold court in any county and may be temporarily assigned to the supreme court in the judicial department of his or her residence or to the county court or the family court in any county or to the surrogate's court in any county outside of the city of New York or to a court for the city of New York established pursuant to section fifteen of this article.

g. A judge of a court for the city of New York established pursuant to section fifteen of this article may perform the duties of office or hold court in any county and may be temporarily assigned to the supreme court in the judicial department of his or her residence or to the county court or the family court in any county or to the other court for the city of New York established pursuant to section fifteen of this article.

h. A judge of the district court in any county may perform the duties of office or hold court in any county and may be temporarily assigned to the county court in the judicial department of his or her residence or to a court for the city of New York established pursuant to section fifteen of this article or to the district court in any county.

i. Temporary assignments of all the foregoing judges or justices listed in this section, and of judges of the city courts pursuant to paragraph two of subdivision j of this section, shall be made by the chief administrator of the courts in accordance with standards and administrative policies established pursuant to section twenty-eight of this article.

j. (1) The legislature may provide for temporary assignments within the county of residence or any adjoining county, of judges of town, village or city courts outside the city of New York.

(2) In addition to any temporary assignments to which a judge of a city court may be subject pursuant to paragraph one of this subdivision, such judge also may be temporarily assigned by the chief administrator of the courts to the county court, the family court or the district court within his or her county of residence or any adjoining county provided he or she is not permitted to practice law.

k. While temporarily assigned pursuant to the provisions of this section, any judge or justice shall have the powers, duties and jurisdiction of a judge or justice of the court to which assigned. After the expiration of any temporary assignment, as provided in this section, the judge or justice assigned shall have all the powers, duties and jurisdiction of a judge or justice of the court to which he or she was assigned with respect to matters pending before him or her during the term of such temporary assignment.

Section 27. Supreme Court; Extraordinary Terms.

The governor may, when in his or her opinion the public interest requires, appoint extraordinary terms of the supreme court. The governor shall designate the time and place of holding the term and the justice who shall hold the term. The governor may terminate the assignment of the justice and may name another justice in his or her place to hold the term.

Section 28. Administrative Supervision of Court System

a. The chief judge of the court of appeals shall be the chief judge of the state of New York and shall be the chief judicial officer of the unified court system. There shall be an administrative board of the courts which shall consist of the chief judge of the court of appeals as chairperson and the presiding justice of the appellate division of the supreme court of each judicial department. The chief judge shall, with the advice and consent of the administrative board of the courts, appoint a chief administrator of the courts who shall serve at the pleasure of the chief judge.

b. The chief administrator, on behalf of the chief judge, shall supervise the administration and operation of the unified court system. In the exercise of such responsibility, the chief administrator of the courts shall have such powers and duties as may be delegated to him or her by the chief judge and such additional powers and duties as may be provided by law.

c. The chief judge, after consultation with the administrative board, shall establish standards and administrative policies for general application throughout the state, which shall be submitted by the chief judge to the court of appeals, together with the recommendations, if any, of the administrative board. Such standards and administrative policies shall be promulgated after approval by the court of appeals.

Section 29. Expenses of Courts

a. The legislature shall provide for the allocation of the cost of operating and maintaining the court of appeals, the appellate division of the supreme court in each judicial department, the supreme court, the court of claims, the county court, the surrogate's court, the family court, the courts for the city of New York established pursuant to section fifteen of this article and the district court, among the state, the counties, the city of New York and other political subdivisions.

b. The legislature shall provide for the submission of the itemized estimates of the annual financial needs of the courts referred to in subdivision a of this section to the chief administrator of the courts to be forwarded to the appropriating bodies with recommendations and comment.

c. Insofar as the expense of the courts is borne by the state or paid by the state in the first instance, the final determination of the itemized estimates of the annual financial needs of the courts shall be made by the legislature and the governor in accordance with articles four and seven of this constitution.

d. Insofar as the expense of the courts is not paid by the state in the first instance and is borne by counties, the city of New York or other political subdivisions, the final determination of the itemized estimates of the annual financial needs of the courts shall be made by the appropriate governing bodies of such counties, the city of New York or other political subdivisions.

Section 30. Legislative Power over Jurisdiction and Proceedings; Delegation of Power to Regulate Practice and Procedure

The legislature shall have the same power to alter and regulate the jurisdiction and proceedings in law and in equity that it has heretofore exercised. The legislature may, on such terms as it shall provide and subject to subsequent modification, delegate, in whole or in part, to a court, including the appellate division of the supreme court, or to the chief administrator of the courts, any power possessed by the legislature to regulate practice and procedure in the courts. The chief administrator of the courts shall exercise any such power delegated to him or her with the advice and consent of the administrative board of the courts. Nothing herein contained shall prevent the adoption of regulations by individual courts consistent with the general practice and procedure as provided by statute or general rules.

Section 31. Inapplicability of Article to Certain Courts
This article does not apply to the peacemakers courts or other Indian courts, the existence and operation of which shall continue as may be provided by law.

Section 32. Custodians of Children to Be of Same Religious Persuasion

When any court having jurisdiction over a child shall commit it or remand it to an institution or agency or place it in the custody of any person by parole, placing out, adoption or guardianship, the child shall be committed or remanded or placed, when practicable, in an institution or agency governed by persons, or in the custody of a person, of the same religious persuasion as the child.

Section 33. Existing Laws; Duty of Legislature to Implement Article

Existing provisions of law not inconsistent with this article shall continue in force until repealed, amended, modified or superseded in accordance with the provisions of this article. The legislature shall enact appropriate laws to carry into effect the purposes and provisions of this article, and may, for the purpose of implementing, supplementing or clarifying any of its provisions, enact any laws, not inconsistent with the provisions of this article, necessary or desirable in promoting the objectives of this article.

Section 34. Pending Appeals, Actions and Proceedings; Preservation of Existing Terms of Office of Judges and Justices

a. The court of appeals, the appellate division of the supreme court, the supreme court, the court of claims, the county court in counties outside the city of New York, the surrogate's court and the district court of Nassau county shall hear and determine all appeals, actions and proceedings pending therein on the effective date of this article except that the appellate division of the supreme court in the first and second judicial departments or the appellate term in such departments, if so directed by the appropriate appellate division of the supreme court, shall hear and determine all appeals pending in the appellate terms of the supreme court in the first and second judicial departments and in the court of special sessions of the city of New York and except that the county court or an appellate term shall, as may be provided by law, hear and determine all appeals pending in the county court or the supreme court other than an appellate term. Further appeal from a decision of the county court, the appellate term or the appellate division of the supreme court, rendered on or after the effective date of this article, shall be governed by the provisions of this article.

b. The justices of the supreme court in office on the effective date of this article shall hold their offices as justices of the supreme court until the expiration of their respective terms.

c. The judges of the court of claims in office on the effective date of this article shall hold their offices as judges of the court of claims until the expiration of their respective terms.

d. The surrogates, and county judges outside the city of New York, including the special county judges of the counties of Erie and Suffolk, in office on the effective date of this article shall hold office as judges of the surrogate's court or county judge, respectively, of such counties until the expiration of their respective terms.

e. The judges of the district court of Nassau county in office on the effective date of this article shall hold their offices until the expiration of their respective terms.

f. Judges of courts for towns, villages and cities outside the city of New York in office on the effective date of this article shall hold their offices until the expiration of their respective terms.

Section 35. Certain Courts Abolished; Transfer of Judges, Court Personnel, and Actions and Proceedings to Other Courts

a. The children's courts, the court of general sessions of the county of New York, the county courts of the counties of Bronx, Kings, Queens and Richmond, the city court of the city of New York, the domestic relations court of the city of New York, the municipal court of the city of New York, the court of special sessions of the city of New York and the city magistrates' courts of the city of New York are abolished from and after the effective date of this article and thereupon the seals, records, papers and documents of or belonging to such courts shall, unless otherwise provided by law, be deposited in the offices of the clerks of the several counties in which these courts now exist.

b. The judges of the county court of the counties of Bronx, Kings, Queens and Richmond and the judges of the court of general sessions of the county of New York in office on the effective date of this article shall, for the remainder of the terms for which they were elected or appointed, be justices of the supreme court in and for the judicial district which includes the county in which they resided on that date. The salaries of such justices shall be the same as the salaries of the other justices of the supreme court residing in the same judicial district and shall be paid in the same manner. All actions and proceedings pending in the county court of the counties of Bronx, Kings, Queens and Richmond and in the court of general sessions of the county of New York on the effective date of this article shall be transferred to the supreme court in the county in which the action or proceedings was pending, or otherwise as may be provided by law.

c. The legislature shall provide by law that the justices of the city court of the city of New York and the justices of the municipal court of the city of New York in office on the date such courts are abolished shall, for the remainder of the term for which each was elected or appointed, be judges of the city-wide court of civil jurisdiction of the city of New York established pursuant to section fifteen of this article and for such district as the legislature may determine.

d. The legislature shall provide by law that the justices of the court of special sessions and the magistrates of the city magistrates' courts of the city of New York in office on the date such courts are abolished shall, for the remainder of the term for which each was appointed, be judges of the city-wide court of criminal jurisdiction of the city of New York established pursuant to section fifteen provided, however, that each term shall expire on the last day of the year in which it would have expired except for the provisions of this article.

e. All actions and proceedings pending in the city court of the city of New York and the municipal court in the city of New York on the date such courts are abolished shall be transferred to the city-wide court of civil jurisdiction of the city of New York established pursuant to section fifteen of this article or as otherwise provided by law.

f. All actions and proceedings pending in the court of special sessions of the city of New York and the city magistrates' courts of the city of New York on the date such courts are abolished shall be transferred to the city-wide court of criminal jurisdiction of the city of New York established pursuant to section fifteen of this article or as otherwise provided by law.

g. The special county judges of the counties of Broome, Chautauqua, Jefferson, Oneida and Rockland and the judges of the children's courts in all counties outside the city of New York in office on the effective date of this article shall, for the remainder of the terms for which they were elected or appointed, be judges of the family court in and for the county in which they hold office. Except as otherwise provided in this section, the office of special county judge and the office of special surrogate is abolished from and after the effective date of this article and the terms of the persons holding such offices shall terminate on that date.

h. All actions and proceedings pending in the children's courts in counties outside the city of New York on the effective date of this article shall be transferred to the family court in the respective counties.

i. The justices of the domestic relations court of the city of New York in office on the effective date of this article shall, for the remainder of the terms for which they were appointed, be judges of the family court within the city of New York.

j. All actions and proceedings pending in the domestic relations court of the city of New York on the effective date of this article shall be transferred to the family court in the city of New York.

k. The office of official referee is abolished, provided, however, that official referees in office on the effective date of this article shall, for the remainder of the terms for which they were appointed or certified, be official referees of the court in which appointed or certified or the successor court, as the case may be. At the expiration of the term of any official referee, his or her office shall be abolished and thereupon such former official referee shall be subject to the relevant provisions of section twenty-five of this article.

l. As may be provided by law, the non-judicial personnel of the courts affected by this article in office on the effective date of this article shall, to the extent practicable, be continued without diminution of salaries and with the same status and rights in the courts established or continued by this article; and especially skilled, experienced and trained personnel shall, to the extent practicable, be assigned to like functions in the courts which exercise the jurisdiction formerly exercised by the courts in which they were employed. In the event that the adoption of this article shall require or make possible a reduction in the number of non-judicial personnel, or in the number of certain categories of such personnel, such reduction shall be made, to the extent practicable, by provision that the death, resignation, removal or retirement of an employee shall not create a vacancy until the reduced number of personnel has been reached.

m. In the event that a judgment or order was entered before the effective date of this article and a right of appeal existed and notice of appeal therefrom is filed after the effective date of this article, such appeal shall be taken from the supreme court, the county courts, the surrogate's courts, the children's courts, the court of general sessions of the county of New York and the domestic relations court of the city of New York to the appellate division of the supreme court in the judicial department in which such court was located; from the court of claims to the appellate division of the supreme court in the third judicial department, except for those claims which arose in the fourth judicial department, in which case the appeal shall be to the appellate division of the supreme court in the fourth judicial department; from the city court of the city of New York, the municipal court of the city of New York, the court of special sessions of the city of New York and the city magistrates' courts of the city of New York to the appellate division of the supreme court in the judicial department in which such court was located, provided, however, that such appellate division of the supreme court may transfer any such appeal to an appellate term, if such appellate term be established; and from the district court, town, village and city courts outside the city of New York to the county court in the county in which such court was located, provided, however, that the legislature may require the transfer of any such appeal to an appellate term, if such appellate term be established. Further appeal from a decision of a county court or an appellate term or the appellate division of the supreme court shall be governed by the provisions of this article. However, if in any action or proceeding decided prior to the effective date of this article, a party had a right of direct appeal from a court of original jurisdiction to the court of appeals, such appeal may be taken directly to the court of appeals.

n. In the event that an appeal was decided before the effective date of this article and a further appeal could be taken as of right and notice of appeal therefrom is filed after the effective date of this article, such appeal may be taken from the appellate division of the supreme court to the court of appeals and from any other court to the appellate division of the supreme court. Further appeal from a decision of the appellate division of the supreme court shall be governed by the provisions of this article. If a further appeal could not be taken as of right, such appeal shall be governed by the provisions of this article.

Section 36. Pending Civil and Criminal Cases

No civil or criminal appeal, action or proceeding pending before any court or any judge or justice on the effective date of this article shall abate but such appeal, action or proceeding so pending shall be continued in the courts as provided in this article and, for the purposes of the disposition of such actions or proceedings only, the jurisdiction of any court to which any such action or proceeding is transferred by this article shall be coextensive with the jurisdiction of the former court from which the action or proceeding was transferred. Except to the extent inconsistent with the provisions of this article, subsequent proceedings in such appeal, action or proceeding shall be conducted in accordance with the laws in force on the effective date of this article until superseded in the manner authorized by law.

Section 36-a. Effective Date of Certain Amendments to Articles VI and VII

The amendments to the provisions of sections two, four, seven, eight, eleven, twenty, twenty-two, twenty-six, twenty-eight, twenty- nine and thirty of article six and to the provisions of section one of article seven, as first proposed by a concurrent resolution passed by the legislature in the year nineteen hundred seventy-six and entitled "Concurrent Resolution of the Senate and Assembly proposing amendments to articles six and seven of the constitution, in relation to the manner of selecting judges of the court of appeals, creation of a commission on judicial conduct and administration of the unified court system, providing for the effectiveness of such amendments and the repeal of subdivision c of section two, subdivision b of section seven, subdivision b of section eleven, section twenty-two and section twenty-eight of article six thereof relating thereto," shall become a part of the constitution on the first day of January next after the approval and ratification of the amendments proposed by such concurrent resolution by the people but the provisions thereof shall not become operative and the repeal of subdivision c of section two, section twenty-two and section twenty-eight shall not become effective until the first day of April next thereafter which date shall be deemed the effective date of such amendments and the chief judge and the associate judges of the court of appeals in office on such effective date shall hold their offices until the expiration of their respective terms. Upon a vacancy in the office of any such judge, such vacancy shall be filled in the manner provided in section two of article six.

Section 36-b.

No Section 36-b

Section 36-c. Effective Date of Certain Amendments to Article VI, Section 22

The amendments to the provisions of section twenty-two of article six as first proposed by a concurrent resolution passed by the legislature in the year nineteen hundred seventy-four and entitled "Concurrent Resolution of the Senate and Assembly proposing an amendment to section twenty-two of article six and adding section thirty-six-c to such article of the constitution, in relation to the powers of and reconstituting the court on the judiciary and creating a commission on judicial conduct," shall become a part of the constitution on the first day of January next after the approval and ratification of the amendments proposed by such concurrent resolution by the people but the provisions thereof shall not become operative until the first day of September next thereafter which date shall be deemed the effective date of such amendments.

Section 37. Effective Date of Article

This article shall become a part of the constitution on the first day of January next after the approval and ratification of this amendment by the people but its provisions shall not become operative until the first day of September next thereafter which date shall be deemed the effective date of this article.

ARTICLE VII: STATE FINANCES

Section 1. Estimates by Departments, the Legislature and the Judiciary of Needed Appropriations; Hearings

For the preparation of the budget, the head of each department of state government, except the legislature and judiciary, shall furnish the governor such estimates and information in such form and at such times as the governor may require, copies of which shall forthwith be furnished to the appropriate committees of the legislature. The governor shall hold hearings thereon at which the governor may require the attendance of heads of departments and their subordinates. Designated representatives of such committees shall be entitled to attend the hearings thereon and to make inquiry concerning any part thereof. Itemized estimates of the financial needs of the legislature, certified by the presiding officer of each house, and of the judiciary, approved by the court of appeals and certified by the chief judge of the court of appeals, shall be transmitted to the governor not later than the first day of December in each year for inclusion in the budget without revision but with such recommendations as the governor may deem proper. Copies of the itemized estimates of the financial needs of the judiciary also shall forthwith be transmitted to the appropriate committees of the legislature.

Section 2. Executive Budget

Annually, on or before the first day of February in each year following the year fixed by the constitution for the election of governor and lieutenant governor, and on or before the second Tuesday following the first day of the annual meeting of the legislature, in all other years, the governor shall submit to the legislature a budget containing a complete plan of expenditures proposed to be made before the close of the ensuing fiscal year and all moneys and revenues estimated to be available therefore, together with an explanation of the basis of such estimates and recommendations as to proposed legislation, if any, which the governor may deem necessary to provide moneys and revenues sufficient to meet such proposed expenditures. It shall also contain such other recommendations and information as the governor may deem proper and such additional information as may be required by law.

Section 3. Budget Bills; Appearances before Legislature

At the time of submitting the budget to the legislature the governor shall submit a bill or bills containing all the proposed appropriations and reappropriations included in the budget and the proposed legislation, if any, recommended therein.
The governor may at any time within thirty days thereafter and, with the consent of the legislature, at any time before the adjournment thereof, amend or supplement the budget and submit amendments to any bills submitted by him or her or submit supplemental bills.

The governor and the heads of departments shall have the right, and it shall be the duty of the heads of departments when requested by either house of the legislature or an appropriate committee thereof, to appear and be heard in respect to the budget during the consideration thereof, and to answer inquiries relevant thereto. The procedure for such appearances and inquiries shall be provided by law.

Section 4. Action on Budget Bills by Legislature; Effect Thereof

The legislature may not alter an appropriation bill submitted by the governor except to strike out or reduce items therein, but it may add thereto items of appropriation provided that such additions are stated separately and distinctly from the original items of the bill and refer each to a single object or purpose. None of the restrictions of this section, however, shall apply to appropriations for the legislature or judiciary.

Such an appropriation bill shall when passed by both houses be a law immediately without further action by the governor, except that appropriations for the legislature and judiciary and separate items added to the governor's bills by the legislature shall be subject to approval of the governor as provided in section 7 of article IV.

Section 5. Restrictions on Consideration of Other Appropriations

Neither house of the legislature shall consider any other bill making an appropriation until all the appropriation bills submitted by the governor shall have been finally acted on by both houses, except on message from the governor certifying to the necessity of the immediate passage of such a bill.

Section 6. Restrictions on Content of Appropriation Bills

Except for appropriations contained in the bills submitted by the governor and in a supplemental appropriation bill for the support of government, no appropriations shall be made except by separate bills each for a single object or purpose. All such bills and such supplemental appropriation bill shall be subject to the governor's approval as provided in section 7 of article IV.
No provision shall be embraced in any appropriation bill submitted by the governor or in such supplemental appropriation bill unless it relates specifically to some particular appropriation in the bill, and any such provision shall be limited in its operation to such appropriation.

Section 7. Appropriation Bills

No money shall ever be paid out of the state treasury or any of its funds, or any of the funds under its management, except in pursuance of an appropriation by law; nor unless such payment be made within two years next after the passage of such appropriation act; and every such law making a new appropriation or continuing or reviving an appropriation, shall distinctly specify the sum appropriated, and the object or purpose to which it is to be applied; and it shall not be sufficient for such law to refer to any other law to fix such sum.

Section 8. Gift or Loan of State Credit or Money Prohibited; Exceptions for Enumerated Purposes

1. The money of the state shall not be given or loaned to or in aid of any private corporation or association, or private undertaking; nor shall the credit of the state be given or loaned to or in aid of any individual, or public or private corporation or association, or private undertaking, but the foregoing provisions shall not apply to any fund or property now held or which may hereafter be held by the state for educational, mental health or mental retardation purposes.

2. Subject to the limitations on indebtedness and taxation, nothing in this constitution contained shall prevent the legislature from providing for the aid, care and support of the needy directly or through subdivisions of the state; or for the protection by insurance or otherwise, against the hazards of unemployment, sickness and old age; or for the education and support of the blind, the deaf, the dumb, the physically handicapped, the mentally ill, the emotionally disturbed, the mentally retarded or juvenile delinquents as it may deem proper; or for health and welfare services for all children, either directly or through subdivisions of the state, including school districts; or for the aid, care and support of neglected and dependent children and of the needy sick, through agencies and institutions authorized by the state board of social welfare or other state department having the power of inspection thereof, by payments made on a per capita basis directly or through the subdivisions of the state; or for the increase in the amount of pensions of any member of a retirement system of the state, or of a subdivision of the state; or for an increase in the amount of pension benefits of any widow or widower of a retired member of a retirement system of the state or of a subdivision of the state to whom payable as beneficiary under an optional settlement in connection with the pension of such member. The enumeration of legislative powers in this paragraph shall not be taken to diminish any power of the legislature hitherto existing.

3. Nothing in this constitution contained shall prevent the legislature from authorizing the loan of the money of the state to a public corporation to be organized for the purpose of making loans to nonprofit corporations or for the purpose of guaranteeing loans made by banking organizations, as that term shall be defined by the legislature, to finance the construction of new industrial or manufacturing plants, the construction of new buildings to be used for research and development, the construction of other eligible business facilities, and for the purchase of machinery and equipment related to such new industrial or manufacturing plants, research and development buildings, and other eligible business facilities in this state or the acquisition, rehabilitation or improvement of former or existing industrial or manufacturing plants, buildings to be used for research and development, other eligible business facilities, and machinery and equipment in this state, including the acquisition of real property therefore, and the use of such money by such public corporation for such purposes, to improve employment opportunities in any area of the state, provided, however, that any such plants, buildings or facilities or machinery and equipment therefore shall not be (i) primarily used in making retail sales of goods or services to customers who personally visit such facilities to obtain such goods or services or (ii) used primarily as a hotel, apartment house or other place of business which furnishes dwelling space or accommodations to either residents or transients, and provided further that any loan by such public corporation shall not exceed sixty per centum of the cost of any such project and the repayment of which shall be secured by a mortgage thereon which shall not be a junior encumbrance thereon by more than fifty per centum of such cost or by a security interest if personalty, and that the amount of any guarantee of a loan made by a banking organization shall not exceed eighty per centum of the cost of any such project.

Section 9. Short Term State Debts in Anticipation of Taxes, Revenues and Proceeds of Sale of Authorized Bonds

The state may contract debts in anticipation of the receipt of taxes and revenues, direct or indirect, for the purposes and within the amounts of appropriations theretofore made. Notes or other obligations for the moneys so borrowed shall be issued as may be provided by law, and shall with the interest thereon be paid from such taxes and revenues within one year from the date of issue.

The state may also contract debts in anticipation of the receipt of the proceeds of the sale of bonds theretofore authorized, for the purpose and within the amounts of the bonds so authorized. Notes or obligations for the money so borrowed shall be issued as may be provided by law, and shall with the interest thereon be paid from the proceeds of the sale of such bonds within two years from the date of issue, except as to bonds issued or to be issued for any of the purposes authorized by article eighteen of this constitution, in which event the notes or obligations shall with the interest thereon be paid from the proceeds of the sale of such bonds within five years from the date of issue.

Section 10. State Debts on Account of Invasion, Insurrection, War and Forest Fires

In addition to the above limited power to contract debts, the state may contract debts to repel invasion, suppress insurrection, or defend the state in war, or to suppress forest fires; but the money arising from the contracting of such debts shall be applied for the purpose for which it was raised, or to repay such debts, and to no other purpose whatever.

Section 11. State Debts Generally; Manner of Contracting; Referendum

Except the debts or refunding debts specified in sections 9, 10 and 13 of this article, no debt shall be hereafter contracted by or in behalf of the state, unless such debt shall be authorized by law, for some single work or purpose, to be distinctly specified therein. No such law shall take effect until it shall, at a general election, have been submitted to the people, and have received a majority of all the votes cast for and against it at such election nor shall it be submitted to be voted on within three months after its passage nor at any general election when any other law or any bill shall be submitted to be voted for or against.
The legislature may, at any time after the approval of such law by the people, if no debt shall have been contracted in pursuance thereof, repeal the same; and may at any time, by law, forbid the contracting of any further debt or liability under such law.

Section 12. State Debts Generally; How Paid; Contribution to Sinking Funds; Restrictions on Use of Bond Proceeds

Except the debts or refunding debts specified in sections 9, 10 and 13 of this article, all debts contracted by the state and each portion of any such debt from time to time so contracted shall be subject to the following rules:

1. The principal of each debt or any portion thereof shall either be paid in equal annual installments or in installments that result in substantially level or declining debt service payments such as shall be authorized by law, or, in the alternative, contributions of principal in the amount that would otherwise be required to be paid annually shall be made to a sinking fund.

2. When some portions of the same debt are payable annually while other portions require contributions to a sinking fund, the entire debt shall be structured so that the combined amount of annual installments of principal paid and/or annual contributions

of principal made in each year shall be equal to the amount that would be required to be paid if the entire debt were payable in annual installments.

3. When interest on state obligations is not paid at least annually, there shall also be contributed to a sinking fund at least annually, the amount necessary to bring the balance thereof, including income earned on contributions, to the accreted value of the obligations to be paid therefrom on the date such contribution is made, less the sum of all required future contributions of principal, in the case of sinking fund obligations, or payments of principal, in the case of serial obligations. Notwithstanding the foregoing, nothing contained in this subdivision shall be deemed to require contributions for interest to sinking funds if total debt service due on the debt or portion thereof in the year such interest is due will be substantially the same as the total debt service due on such debt or portion thereof in each other year or if the total amount of debt service due in each subsequent year on such debt or portion thereof shall be less than the total debt service due in each prior year.

4. The first annual installment on such debt shall be paid, or the first annual contribution shall be made to a sinking fund, not more than one year, and the last installment shall be paid, or contribution made not more than forty years, after such debt or portion thereof shall have been contracted, provided, however, that in contracting any such debt the privilege of paying all or any part of such debt prior to the date on which the same shall be due may be reserved to the state in such manner as may be provided by law.

5. No such debt shall be contracted for a period longer than that of the probable life of the work or purpose for which the debt is to be contracted, or in the alternative, the weighted average period of probable life of the works or purposes for which such indebtedness is to be contracted. The probable lives of such works or purposes shall be determined by general laws, which determination shall be conclusive.

6. The money arising from any loan creating such debt or liability shall be applied only to the work or purpose specified in the act authorizing such debt or liability, or for the payment of such debt or liability, including any notes or obligations issued in anticipation of the sale of bonds evidencing such debt or liability.

7. Any sinking funds created pursuant to this section shall be maintained and managed by the state comptroller or an agent or trustee designated by the state comptroller, and amounts in sinking funds created pursuant to this section, and earnings thereon, shall be used solely for the purpose of retiring the obligations secured thereby except that amounts in excess of the required balance on any contribution date and amounts remaining in such funds after all of the obligations secured thereby have been retired shall be deposited in the general fund.

8. No appropriation shall be required for disbursement of money, or income earned thereon, from any sinking fund created pursuant to this section for the purpose of paying principal of and interest on the obligations for which such fund was created, except that interest shall be paid from any such fund only if, and to the extent that, it is not payable annually and contributions on account of such interest were made thereto.

9. The provisions of section 15 of this article shall not apply to sinking funds created pursuant to this section.

10. When state obligations are sold at a discount, the debt incurred for purposes of determining the amount of debt issued or outstanding pursuant to a voter approved bond referendum or other limitation on the amount of debt that may be issued or outstanding for a work or purpose shall be deemed to include only the amount of money actually received by the state notwithstanding the face amount of such obligations.

Section 13. Refund of State Debts

The legislature may provide means and authority whereby any state debt or debts, or any portion or combination thereof, may be refunded in accordance with the following provisions:

1. State debts may be refunded at any time after they are incurred provided that the state will achieve a debt service savings on a present value basis as a result of the refunding transaction, and further provided that no maturity shall be called for redemption unless the privilege to pay prior to the maturity date was reserved to the state. The legislature may provide for the method of computation of present value for such purpose.

2. In no event shall refunding obligations be issued in an amount exceeding that necessary to provide sufficient funds to accomplish the refunding of the obligations to be refunded including paying all costs and expenses related to the refunding transaction and, in no event, shall the proceeds of refunding obligations be applied to any purpose other than accomplishing the refunding of the debt to be refunded and paying costs and expenses related to the refunding.

3. Proceeds of refunding obligations shall be deposited in escrow funds which shall be maintained and managed by the state comptroller or by an agent or trustee designated by the state comptroller and no legislative appropriation shall be required for disbursement of money, or income earned thereon, from such escrow funds for the purposes enumerated in this section.

4. Refunding obligations may be refunded pursuant to this section.

5. Refunding obligations shall either be paid in annual installments or annual contributions shall be made to a sinking fund in amounts sufficient to retire the refunding obligations at their maturity. No annual installments or contributions of principal need be made with respect to all or any portion of an issue of refunding obligations in years when debt service on such refunding obligations or portion thereof is paid or contributed entirely from an escrow fund created pursuant to subdivision 3 of this section or in years when no installments or contributions would have been due on the obligations to be refunded. So long as any of the refunding obligations remain outstanding, installments or contributions shall be made in any years that installments or contributions would have been due on the obligations to be refunded.

6. In no event shall the last annual installment or contribution on any portion of refunding debt, including refunding obligations issued to refund other refunding obligations, be made after the termination of the period of probable life of the projects financed with the proceeds of the relevant portion of the debt to be refunded, or any debt previously refunded with the refunding obligations to be refunded, determined as of the date of issuance of the original obligations pursuant to section 12 of this article to finance such projects, or forty years from such date, if earlier; provided, however, that in lieu of the foregoing, an entire refunding issue or portion thereof may be structured to mature over the remaining weighted average useful life of all projects financed with the obligations being refunded.

7. Subject to the provisions of subdivision 5 of this section, each annual installment or contribution of principal of refunding obligations shall be equal to the amount that would be required by subdivision 1 of section 12 of this article if such installments or contributions were required to be made from the year that the next installment or contribution would have been due on the obligations to be refunded, if they had not been refunded, until the final maturity of the refunding obligations but excluding any year in which no installment or contribution would have been due on the obligations to be refunded or, in the alternative, the total payments of principal and interest on the refunding bonds shall be less in each year to their final maturity than the total payments of principal and interest on the bonds to be refunded in each such year.

8. The provisions of subdivision 3 and subdivisions 7 through 9 of section 12 of this article shall apply to sinking funds created pursuant to this section for the payment at maturity of refunding obligations.

Section 14. State Debt for Elimination of Railroad Crossings at Grade; Expenses; How Borne; Construction and Reconstruction of State Highways and Parkways

The legislature may authorize by law the creation of a debt or debts of the state, not exceeding in the aggregate three hundred million dollars, to provide moneys for the elimination, under state supervision, of railroad crossings at grade within the state, and for incidental improvements connected therewith as authorized by this section. The provisions of this article, not inconsistent with this section, relating to the issuance of bonds for a debt or debts of the state and the maturity and payment thereof, shall apply to a state debt or debts created pursuant to this section; except that the law authorizing the contracting of such debt or debts shall take effect without submission to the people pursuant to section 11 of this article. The aggregate amount of a state debt or debts which may be created pursuant to this section shall not exceed the difference between the amount of the debt or debts heretofore created or authorized by law, under the provisions of section 14 of article VII of the constitution in force on July first, nineteen hundred thirty-eight, and the sum of three hundred million dollars.

The expense of any grade crossing elimination the construction work for which was not commenced before January first, nineteen hundred thirty-nine, including incidental improvements connected therewith as authorized by this section, whether or not an order for such elimination shall theretofore have been made, shall be paid by the state in the first instance, but the state shall be entitled to recover from the railroad company or companies, by way of reimbursement:

(1) the entire amount of the railroad improvements not an essential part of elimination, and

(2) the amount of the net benefit to the company or companies from the elimination exclusive of such railroad improvements, the amount of such net benefit to be adjudicated after the completion of the work in the manner to be prescribed by law, and in no event to exceed fifteen per centum of the expense of the elimination, exclusive of all incidental improvements. The reimbursement by the railroad companies shall be payable at such times, in such manner and with interest at such rate as the legislature may prescribe.

The expense of any grade crossing elimination the construction work for which was commenced before January first, nineteen hundred thirty-nine, shall be borne by the state, railroad companies, and the municipality or municipalities in the proportions formerly prescribed by section 14 of article VII of the constitution in force on July first, nineteen hundred thirty-eight, and the law or laws enacted pursuant to its provisions, applicable to such elimination, and subject to the provisions of such former section and law or laws, including advances in aid of any railroad company or municipality, although such elimination shall not be completed until after January first, nineteen hundred thirty-nine. A grade crossing elimination the construction work for which shall be commenced after January first, nineteen hundred thirty-nine, shall include incidental improvements rendered necessary or desirable because of such elimination, and reasonably included in the engineering plans therefore. Out of the balance of all moneys authorized to be expended under section 14 of article VII of the constitution in force on July first, nineteen hundred thirty-eight, and remaining unexpended and unobligated on such date, fifty million dollars shall be deemed segregated for grade crossing eliminations and incidental improvements in the city of New York and shall be available only for such purposes until such eliminations and improvements are completed and paid for. Notwithstanding any of the foregoing provisions of this section the legislature is hereby authorized to appropriate, out of the proceeds of bonds now or hereafter sold to provide moneys for the elimination of railroad crossings at grade and incidental improvements pursuant to this section, sums not exceeding in the aggregate sixty million dollars for the construction and reconstruction of state highways and parkways.

Section 15. Sinking Funds; How Kept and Invested; Income Therefrom and Application Thereof

The sinking funds provided for the payment of interest and the extinguishment of the principal of the debts of the state heretofore contracted shall be continued; they shall be separately kept and safely invested, and neither of them shall be appropriated or used in any manner other than for such payment and extinguishment as hereinafter provided. The comptroller shall each year appraise the securities held for investment in each of such funds at their fair market value not exceeding par. The comptroller shall then determine and certify to the legislature the amount of each of such funds and the amounts which, if thereafter annually contributed to each such fund, would, with the fund and with the accumulations thereon and upon the contributions thereto, computed at the rate of three per centum per annum, produce at the date of maturity the amount of the debt to retire which such fund was created, and the legislature shall thereupon appropriate as the contribution to each such fund for such year at least the amount thus certified. If the income of any such fund in any year is more than a sum which, if annually added to such fund would, with the fund and its accumulations as aforesaid, retire the debt at maturity, the excess income may be applied to the interest on the debt for which the fund was created.

After any sinking fund shall equal in amount the debt for which it was created no further contribution shall be made thereto except to make good any losses ascertained at the annual appraisals above mentioned, and the income thereof shall be applied to the payment of the interest on such debt. Any excess in such income not required for the payment of interest may be applied to the general fund of the state.

Section 16. Payment of State Debts; When Comptroller to Pay without Appropriation

The legislature shall annually provide by appropriation for the payment of the interest upon and installments of principal of all debts or refunding debts created on behalf of the state except those contracted under section 9 of this article, as the same shall fall due, and for the contribution to all of the sinking funds created by law, of the amounts annually to be contributed under the provisions of section 12, 13 or 15 of this article. If at any time the legislature shall fail to make any such appropriation, the comptroller shall set apart from the first revenues thereafter received, applicable to the general fund of the state, a sum sufficient to pay such interest, installments of principal, or contributions to such sinking fund, as the case may be, and shall so apply the moneys thus set apart. The comptroller may be required to set aside and apply such revenues as aforesaid, at the suit of any holder of such bonds.

Notwithstanding the foregoing provisions of this section, the comptroller may covenant with the purchasers of any state obligations that they shall have no further rights against the state for payment of such obligations or any interest thereon after an amount or amounts determined in accordance with the provisions of such covenant is deposited in a described fund or with a named or described agency or trustee. In such case, this section shall have no further application with respect to payment of such obligations or any interest thereon after the comptroller has complied with the prescribed conditions of such covenant.

Section 17. Authorizing the Legislature to Establish a Fund or Funds for Tax Revenue Stabilization Reserves; Regulating Payments Thereto and Withdrawals Therefrom

The legislature may establish a fund or funds to aid in the stabilization of the tax revenues of the state available for

expenditure or distribution. Any law creating such a fund shall specify the tax or taxes to which such fund relates, and shall prescribe the method of determining the amount of revenue from any such tax or taxes which shall constitute a norm of each fiscal year. Such part as shall be prescribed by law of any revenue derived from such tax or taxes during a fiscal year in excess of such norm shall be paid into such fund. No moneys shall at any time be withdrawn from such fund unless the revenue derived from such tax or taxes during a fiscal year shall fall below the norm for such year; in which event such amount as may be prescribed by law, but in no event an amount exceeding the difference between such revenue and such norm, shall be paid from such fund into the general fund.
No law changing the method of determining a norm or prescribing the amount to be paid into such a fund or to be paid from such a fund into the general fund may become effective until three years from the date of its enactment.

Section 18. Bonus on Account of Service of Certain Veterans in World War II

The legislature may authorize by law the creation of a debt or debts of the state to provide for the payment of a bonus to each male and female member of the armed forces of the United States, still in the armed forces, or separated or discharged under honorable conditions, for service while on active duty with the armed forces at any time during the period from December seventh, nineteen hundred forty-one to and including September second, nineteen hundred forty-five, who was a resident of this state for a period of at least six months immediately prior to his or her enlistment, induction or call to active duty. The law authorizing the creation of the debt shall provide for payment of such bonus to the next of kin of each male and female member of the armed forces who, having been a resident of this state for a period of six months immediately prior to his or her enlistment, induction or call to active duty, died while on active duty at any time during the period from December seventh, nineteen hundred forty-one to and including September second, nineteen hundred forty-five; or who died while on active duty subsequent to September second, nineteen hundred forty-five, or after his or her separation or discharge under honorable conditions, prior to receiving payment of such bonus. An apportionment of the moneys on the basis of the periods and places of service of such members of the armed forces shall be provided by general laws. The aggregate of the debts authorized by this section shall not exceed four hundred million dollars. The provisions of this article, not inconsistent with this section, relating to the issuance of bonds for a debt or debts of the state and the maturity and payment thereof, shall apply to a debt or debts created pursuant to this section; except that the law authorizing the contracting of such debt or debts shall take effect without submission to the people pursuant to section eleven of this article.

Proceeds of bonds issued pursuant to law, as authorized by this section as in force prior to January first, nineteen hundred fifty shall be available and may be expended for the payment of such bonus to persons qualified therefore as now provided by this section.

Section 19. State Debt for Expansion of State University

The legislature may authorize by law the creation of a debt or debts of the state, not exceeding in the aggregate two hundred fifty million dollars, to provide moneys for the construction, reconstruction, rehabilitation, improvement and equipment of facilities for the expansion and development of the program of higher education provided and to be provided at institutions now or hereafter comprised within the state university, for acquisition of real property therefore, and for payment of the state's share of the capital costs of locally sponsored institutions of higher education approved and regulated by the state university trustees. The provisions of this article, not inconsistent with this section, relating to the issuance of bonds for a debt or debts of the state and the maturity and payment thereof, shall apply to a state debt or debts created pursuant to this section; except that the law authorizing the contracting of such debt or debts shall take effect without submission to the people pursuant to section eleven of this article.

ARTICLE VIII: LOCAL FINANCES

Section 1. Gift or Loan of Property or Credit of Local Subdivisions Prohibited; Exceptions for Enumerated Purposes
No county, city, town, village or school district shall give or loan any money or property to or in aid of any individual, or private corporation or association, or private undertaking, or become directly or indirectly the owner of stock in, or bonds of, any private corporation or association; nor shall any county, city, town, village or school district give or loan its credit to or in aid of any individual, or public or private corporation or association, or private undertaking, except that two or more such units may join together pursuant to law in providing any municipal facility, service, activity or undertaking which each of such units has the power to provide separately. Each such unit may be authorized by the legislature to contract joint or several indebtedness, pledge its or their faith and credit for the payment of such indebtedness for such joint undertaking and levy real estate or other authorized taxes or impose charges therefore subject to the provisions of this constitution otherwise restricting the power of such units to contract indebtedness or to levy taxes on real estate. The legislature shall have power to provide by law for the manner and the proportion in which indebtedness arising out of such joint undertakings shall be incurred by such units and shall have power to provide a method by which such indebtedness shall be determined, allocated and apportioned among such units and such indebtedness treated for purposes of exclusion from applicable constitutional limitations, provided that in no event shall more than the total amount of indebtedness incurred for such joint undertaking be included in ascertaining the power of all such participating units to incur indebtedness. Such law may provide that such determination, allocation and apportionment shall be conclusive if made or approved by the comptroller. This provision shall not prevent a county from contracting indebtedness for the purpose of advancing to a town or school district, pursuant to law, the amount of unpaid taxes returned to it.

Subject to the limitations on indebtedness and taxation applying to any county, city, town or village nothing in this constitution contained shall prevent a county, city or town from making such provision for the aid, care and support of the needy as may be authorized by law, nor prevent any such county, city or town from providing for the care, support, maintenance and secular education of inmates of orphan asylums, homes for dependent children or correctional institutions and of children placed in family homes by authorized agencies, whether under public or private control, or from providing health and welfare services for all children, nor shall anything in this constitution contained prevent a county, city, town or village from increasing the pension benefits payable to retired members of a police department or fire department or to widows, dependent children or dependent parents of members or retired members of a police department or fire department; or prevent the city of New York from increasing the pension benefits payable to widows, dependent children or dependent parents of members or retired members of the relief and pension fund of the department of street cleaning of the city of New York. Payments by counties, cities or towns to charitable, eleemosynary, correctional and reformatory institutions and agencies, wholly or partly under private control, for care, support and maintenance, may be authorized, but shall not be required, by the legislature. No such payments shall be made for any person cared for by any such institution or agency, nor for a child placed in a family home, who is not received and retained therein pursuant to rules established by the state board of social welfare or other state department having the power of inspection thereof.

Section 2. Restrictions on Indebtedness of Local Subdivisions; Contracting and Payment of Local Indebtedness; Exceptions

No county, city, town, village or school district shall contract any indebtedness except for county, city, town, village or school district purposes, respectively. No indebtedness shall be contracted for longer than the period of probable usefulness of the object or purpose for which such indebtedness is to be

contracted, or, in the alternative, the weighted average period of probable usefulness of the several objects or purposes for which such indebtedness is to be contracted, to be determined by the governing body of the county, city, town, village or school district contracting such indebtedness pursuant to general or special laws of the state legislature, which determination shall be conclusive, and in no event for longer than forty years. Indebtedness or any portion thereof may be refunded within either such period of probable usefulness, or average period of probable usefulness, as may be determined by such governing body computed from the date such indebtedness was contracted. No indebtedness shall be contracted by any county, city, town, village or school district unless such county, city, town, village or school district shall have pledged its faith and credit for the payment of the principal thereof and the interest thereon. Except for indebtedness contracted in anticipation of the collection of taxes actually levied and uncollected or to be levied for the year when such indebtedness is contracted and indebtedness contracted to be paid in one of the two fiscal years immediately succeeding the fiscal year in which such indebtedness was contracted, all such indebtedness and each portion thereof from time to time contracted, including any refunding thereof, shall be paid in annual installments, the first of which, except in the case of refunding of indebtedness heretofore contracted, shall be paid not more than two years after such indebtedness or portion thereof shall have been contracted, and no installment, except in the case of refunding of indebtedness heretofore contracted, shall be more than fifty per centum in excess of the smallest prior installment, unless the governing body of the county, city, town, village or school district contracting such indebtedness provides for substantially level or declining debt service payments as may be authorized by law.
Notwithstanding the foregoing provisions, indebtedness contracted by the city of New York and each portion of any such indebtedness from time to time so contracted for the supply of water, including the acquisition of land in connection with such purpose, may be financed either by serial bonds with a maximum maturity of fifty years, in which case such indebtedness shall be

paid in annual installments as hereinbefore provided, or by sinking fund bonds with a maximum maturity of fifty years, which shall be redeemed through annual contributions to sinking funds established and maintained for the purpose of amortizing the indebtedness for which such bonds are issued. Notwithstanding the foregoing provisions, indebtedness hereafter contracted by the city of New York and each portion of any such indebtedness from time to time so contracted for

(a) the acquisition, construction or equipment of rapid transit railroads, or

(b) the construction of docks, including the acquisition of land in connection with any of such purposes, may be financed either by serial bonds with a maximum maturity of forty years, in which case such indebtedness shall be paid in annual installments as hereinbefore provided, or by sinking fund bonds with a maximum maturity of forty years, which shall be redeemed through annual contributions to sinking funds established and maintained for the purpose of amortizing the indebtedness for which such bonds are issued.

Notwithstanding the foregoing provisions, but subject to such requirements as the legislature shall impose by general or special law, indebtedness contracted by any county, city, town, village or school district and each portion thereof from time to time contracted for any object or purpose for which indebtedness may be contracted may also be financed by sinking fund bonds with a maximum maturity of fifty years, which shall be redeemed through annual contributions to sinking funds established by such county, city, town, village or school district, provided, however, that each such annual contribution shall be at least equal to the amount required, if any, to enable the sinking fund to redeem, on the date of the contribution, the same amount of such indebtedness as would have been paid and then be payable if such indebtedness had been financed entirely by the issuance of serial bonds, except, if an issue of sinking fund bonds is combined for sale with an issue of serial bonds, for the same object or purpose, then the amount of each annual sinking fund contribution shall be at least equal to the amount required, if any, to enable the sinking fund to redeem, on the date of each such annual contribution, (i) the amount which would be required to be paid annually if such indebtedness had been issued entirely as serial bonds, less (ii) the amount of indebtedness, if any, to be paid during such year on the portion of such indebtedness actually issued as serial bonds. Sinking funds established on or after January first, nineteen hundred eighty-six pursuant to the preceding sentence shall be maintained and managed by the state comptroller pursuant to such requirements and procedures as the legislature shall prescribe, including provisions for reimbursement by the issuer of bonds payable from such sinking funds for the expenses related to such maintenance and management.

Provisions shall be made annually by appropriation by every county, city, town, village and school district for the payment of interest on all indebtedness and for the amounts required for

(a) the amortization and redemption of term bonds, sinking fund bonds and serial bonds,

(b) the redemption of certificates or other evidence of indebtedness (except those issued in anticipation of the collection of taxes or other revenues, or renewals thereof, and which are described in paragraph A of section five of this article and those issued in anticipation of the receipt of the proceeds of the sale of bonds theretofore authorized) contracted to be paid in such year out of the tax levy or other revenues applicable to a reduction thereof, and

(c) the redemption of certificates or other evidence of indebtedness issued in anticipation of the collection of taxes or other revenues, or renewals thereof, which are not retired within five years after their date of original issue. If at any time the respective appropriating authorities shall fail to make such appropriations, a sufficient sum shall be set apart from the first revenues thereafter received and shall be applied to such purposes. The fiscal officer of any county, city, town, village or school district may be required to set apart and apply such revenues as aforesaid at the suit of any holder of obligations issued for any such indebtedness.

Notwithstanding the foregoing, all interest need not be paid annually on an issue of indebtedness provided that either

(a) substantially level or declining debt service payments (including all payments of interest) shall be made over the life of such issue of indebtedness, or

(b) there shall annually be contributed to a sinking fund created pursuant to this section, the amount necessary to bring the balance thereof, including income earned on contributions, to the accreted value of the obligations to be paid therefrom on the date such contribution is made, less the sum of all required future contributions of principal, in the case of sinking fund obligations, or payments of principal, in the case of serial obligations. When obligations are sold by a county, city, town, village or school district at a discount, the debt incurred for the purposes of any debt limitation contained in this constitution, shall be deemed to include only the amount of money actually received by the county, city, town, village or school district, irrespective of the face amount of the obligations.

Section 2-a. Local Indebtedness for Water Supply, Sewage and Drainage Facilities and Purposes; Allocations and Exclusions of Indebtedness

Notwithstanding the provisions of section one of this article, the legislature by general or special law and subject to such conditions as it shall impose:

A. May authorize any county, city, town or village or any county or town on behalf of an improvement district to contract indebtedness to provide a supply of water, in excess of its own needs, for sale to any other public corporation or improvement district;

B. May authorize two or more public corporations and improvement districts to provide for a common supply of water and may authorize any such corporation, or any county or town on behalf of an improvement district, to contract joint indebtedness for such purpose or to contract indebtedness for specific proportions of the cost;

C. May authorize any county, city, town or village or any county or town on behalf of an improvement district to contract indebtedness to provide facilities, in excess of its own needs, for the conveyance, treatment and disposal of sewage from any other public corporation or improvement district;

D. May authorize two or more public corporations and improvement districts to provide for the common conveyance, treatment and disposal of sewage and may authorize any such corporation, or any county or town on behalf of an improvement district, to contract joint indebtedness for such purpose or to contract indebtedness for specific proportions of the cost;

E. May authorize any county, city, town or village or any county or town on behalf of an improvement district to contract indebtedness to provide facilities, in excess of its own needs, for drainage purposes from any other public corporation or improvement district.

F. May authorize two or more public corporations and improvement districts to provide for a common drainage system and may authorize any such corporation, or any county or town on behalf of an improvement district, to contract joint indebtedness for such purpose or to contract indebtedness for specific proportions of the cost.

Indebtedness contracted by a county, city, town or village pursuant to this section shall be for a county, city, town or village purpose, respectively. In ascertaining the power of a county, city, town or village to contract indebtedness, any indebtedness contracted pursuant to paragraphs A and B of this section shall be excluded.

The legislature shall provide the method by which a fair proportion of joint indebtedness contracted pursuant to paragraphs D and F of this section shall be allocated to any county, city, town or village.

The legislature by general law in terms and in effect applying alike to all counties, to all cities, to all towns and/or to all villages also may provide that all or any part of indebtedness contracted or proposed to be contracted by any county, city, town or village pursuant to paragraphs D and F of this section for a revenue producing public improvement or service may be excluded periodically in ascertaining the power of such county, city, town or village to contract indebtedness. The amount of any such exclusion shall have a reasonable relation to the extent to which such public improvement or service shall have yielded or is expected to yield revenues sufficient to provide for the payment of the interest on and amortization of or payment of indebtedness contracted or proposed to be contracted for such public improvement or service, after deducting all costs of operation, maintenance and repairs thereof. The legislature shall provide the method by which a fair proportion of joint indebtedness proposed to be contracted pursuant to paragraphs D and F of this section shall be allocated to any county, city, town or village for the purpose of determining the amount of any such exclusion. The provisions of paragraph C of section five and section ten-a of this article shall not apply to indebtedness contracted pursuant to paragraphs D and F of this section.
The legislature may provide that any allocation of indebtedness, or determination of the amount of any exclusion of indebtedness, made pursuant to this section shall be conclusive if made or approved by the state comptroller.

Section 3. Restrictions on Creation and Indebtedness of Certain Corporations

No municipal or other corporation (other than a county, city, town, village, school district or fire district, or a river improvement, river regulating, or drainage district, established by or under the supervision of the department of conservation) possessing the power

(a) to contract indebtedness and

(b) to levy taxes or benefit assessments upon real estate or to require the levy of such taxes or assessments, shall hereafter be established or created, but nothing herein shall prevent the creation of improvement districts in counties and towns, provided that the county or town or towns in which such districts are located shall pledge its or their faith and credit for the payment of the principal of and interest on all indebtedness to be contracted for the purposes of such districts, and in ascertaining the power of any such county or town to contract indebtedness, such indebtedness shall be included, unless such indebtedness would, under the provisions of this article, be excluded in ascertaining the power of a county or town to contract indebtedness. No such corporation now existing shall hereafter contract any indebtedness without the consent, granted in such manner as may be prescribed by general law, of the city or village within which, or of the town within any unincorporated area of which any real estate may be subject to such taxes or assessments. If the real estate subject to such taxes or assessments is wholly within a city, village or the unincorporated area of a town, in ascertaining the power of such city, village or town to contract indebtedness, there shall be included any indebtedness hereafter contracted by such corporation, unless such indebtedness would, under the provisions of this article, be excluded if contracted by such city, village or town. If only part of the real estate subject to such taxes or assessments is within a city, village or the unincorporated area of a town, in ascertaining the power of such city, village or town to contract indebtedness, there shall be included the proportion, determined as prescribed by general law, of any indebtedness hereafter contracted by such corporation, unless such indebtedness would, under the provisions of this article, be excluded if contracted by such city, village or town.

Section 4. Limitations on Local Indebtedness

Except as otherwise provided in this constitution, no county, city, town, village or school district described in this section shall be allowed to contract indebtedness for any purpose or in any manner which, including existing indebtedness, shall exceed an amount equal to the following percentages of the average full valuation of taxable real estate of such county, city, town, village or school district:

(a) the county of Nassau, for county purposes, ten per centum;

(b) any county, other than the county of Nassau, for county purposes, seven per centum;

(c) the city of New York, for city purposes, ten per centum;

(d) any city, other than the city of New York, having one hundred twenty-five thousand or more inhabitants according to the latest federal census, for city purposes, nine per centum;

(e) any city having less than one hundred twenty-five thousand inhabitants according to the latest federal census, for city purposes, excluding education purposes, seven per centum;

(f) any town, for town purposes, seven per centum;

(g) any village for village purposes, seven per centum; and

(h) any school district which is coterminous with, or partly within, or wholly within, a city having less than one hundred twenty-five thousand inhabitants according to the latest federal census, for education purposes, five per centum; provided, however, that such limitation may be increased in relation to indebtedness for specified objects or purposes with

(1) the approving vote of sixty per centum or more of the duly qualified voters of such school district voting on a proposition therefore submitted at a general or special election,

(2) the consent of The Regents of the University of the State of New York and

(3) the consent of the state comptroller. The legislature shall prescribe by law the qualifications for voting at any such election. Except as otherwise provided in this constitution, any indebtedness contracted in excess of the respective limitations prescribed in this section shall be void.

In ascertaining the power of any city having less than one hundred twenty-five thousand inhabitants according to the latest federal census to contract indebtedness, indebtedness heretofore contracted by such city for education purposes shall be excluded. Such indebtedness so excluded shall be included in ascertaining the power of a school district which is coterminous with, or partly within, or wholly within, such city to contract indebtedness. The legislature shall prescribe by law the manner by which the amount of such indebtedness shall be determined and allocated among such school districts. Such law may provide that such determinations and allocations shall be conclusive if made or approved by the state comptroller.

In ascertaining the power of a school district described in this section to contract indebtedness, certificates or other evidences of indebtedness described in paragraph A of section five of this article shall be excluded.

The average full valuation of taxable real estate of any such county, city, town, village or school district shall be determined in the manner prescribed in section ten of this article.
Nothing contained in this section shall be deemed to restrict the powers granted to the legislature by other provisions of this constitution to further restrict the powers of any county, city, town, village or school district to contract indebtedness.

Section 5. Ascertainment of Debt-Incurring Power of Counties, Cities, Towns and Villages; Certain Indebtedness to Be Excluded

In ascertaining the power of a county, city, town or village to contract indebtedness, there shall be excluded:

A. Certificates or other evidences of indebtedness (except serial bonds of an issue having a maximum maturity of more than two years) issued for purposes other than the financing of capital improvements and contracted to be redeemed in one of the two fiscal years immediately succeeding the year of their issue, and certificates or other evidences of indebtedness issued in any fiscal year in anticipation of (a) the collection of taxes on real estate for amounts theretofore actually levied and uncollected or to be levied in such year and payable out of such taxes, (b) moneys receivable from the state which have theretofore been apportioned by the state or which are to be so apportioned within one year after their issue and (c) the collection of any other taxes due and payable or to become due and payable within one year or of other revenues to be received within one year after their issue; excepting any such certificates or other evidences of indebtedness or renewals thereof which are not retired within five years after their date of original issue.

B. Indebtedness heretofore or hereafter contracted to provide for the supply of water.

C. Indebtedness heretofore or hereafter contracted by any county, city, town or village for a public improvement or part thereof, or service, owned or rendered by such county, city, town or village, annually proportionately to the extent that the same shall have yielded to such county, city, town or village net revenue; provided, however, that such net revenue shall be twenty-five per centum or more of the amount required in such year for the payment of the interest on, amortization of, or payment of, such indebtedness. Such exclusion shall be granted only if the revenues of such public improvement or part thereof, or service, are applied to and actually used for payment of all costs of operation, maintenance and repairs, and payment of the amounts required in such year for interest on and amortization of or redemption of such indebtedness, or such revenues are deposited in a special fund to be used solely for such payments. Any revenues remaining after such payments are made may be used for any lawful purpose of such county, city, town or village, respectively.

Net revenue shall be determined by deducting from gross revenues of the preceding year all costs of operation, maintenance and repairs for such year, or the legislature may provide that net revenue shall be determined by deducting from the average of the gross revenues of not to exceed five of the preceding years during which the public improvement or part thereof, or service, has been in operation, the average of all costs of operation, maintenance and repairs for the same years. A proportionate exclusion of indebtedness contracted or proposed to be contracted also may be granted for the period from the date when such indebtedness is first contracted or to be contracted for such public improvement or part thereof, or service, through the first year of operation of such public improvement or part thereof, or service. Such exclusion shall be computed in the manner provided in this section on the basis of estimated net revenue which shall be determined by deducting from the gross revenues estimated to be received during the first year of operation of such public improvement or part thereof, or service, all estimated costs of operation, maintenance and repairs for such year. The amount of any such proportionate exclusion shall not exceed seventy-five per centum of the amount which would be excluded if the computation were made on the basis of net revenue instead of estimated net revenue. Except as otherwise provided herein, the legislature shall prescribe the method by which and the terms and conditions under which the proportionate amount of any such indebtedness to be so excluded shall be determined and no proportionate amount of such indebtedness shall be excluded except in accordance with such determination. The legislature may provide that the state comptroller shall make such determination or it may confer appropriate jurisdiction on the appellate division of the supreme court in the judicial departments in which such counties, cities, towns or villages are located for the purpose of determining the proportionate amount of any such indebtedness to be so excluded.

The provisions of this paragraph C shall not affect or impair any existing exclusions of indebtedness, or the power to exclude indebtedness, granted by any other provision of this constitution.

D. Serial bonds, issued by any county, city, town or village which now maintains a pension or retirement system or fund which is not on an actuarial reserve basis with current payments to the reserve adequate to provide for all current accruing liabilities. Such bonds shall not exceed in the aggregate an amount sufficient to provide for the payment of the liabilities of such system or fund, accrued on the date of issuing such bonds, both on account of pensioners on the pension roll on that date and prospective pensions to dependents of such pensioners and on account of prior service of active members of such system or fund on that date. Such bonds or the proceeds thereof shall be deposited in such system or fund. Each such pension or retirement system or fund thereafter shall be maintained on an actuarial reserve basis with current payments to the reserve adequate to provide for all current accruing liabilities.

E. Indebtedness contracted on or after January first, nineteen hundred sixty-two and prior to January first, two thousand twenty-four, for the construction or reconstruction of facilities for the conveyance, treatment and disposal of sewage. The legislature shall prescribe the method by which and the terms and conditions under which the amount of any such indebtedness to be excluded shall be determined, and no such indebtedness shall be excluded except in accordance with such determination.

Section 6. Debt-Incurring Power of Buffalo, Rochester and Syracuse; Certain Additional Indebtedness to be Excluded

In ascertaining the power of the cities of Buffalo, Rochester and Syracuse to contract indebtedness, in addition to the indebtedness excluded by section 5 of this article, there shall be excluded:

Indebtedness not exceeding in the aggregate the sum of ten million dollars, heretofore or hereafter contracted by the city of Buffalo or the city of Rochester and indebtedness not exceeding in the aggregate the sum of five million dollars heretofore or hereafter contracted by the city of Syracuse for so much of the cost and expense of any public improvement as may be required by the ordinance or other local law therein assessing the same to be raised by assessment upon local property or territory.

Section 7. Debt-Incurring Power of New York City; Certain Additional Indebtedness to Be Excluded

In ascertaining the power of the city of New York to contract indebtedness, in addition to the indebtedness excluded by section 5 of this article, there shall be excluded:

A. Indebtedness contracted prior to the first day of January, nineteen hundred ten, for dock purposes proportionately to the extent to which the current net revenues received by the city therefrom shall meet the interest on and the annual requirements for the amortization of such indebtedness. The legislature shall prescribe the method by which and the terms and conditions under which the amount of any such indebtedness to be so excluded shall be determined, and no such indebtedness shall be excluded except in accordance with such determination. The legislature may confer appropriate jurisdiction on the appellate division of the supreme court in the first judicial department for the purpose of determining the amount of any such indebtedness to be so excluded.

B. The aggregate of indebtedness initially contracted from time to time after January first, nineteen hundred twenty-eight, for the construction or equipment, or both, of new rapid transit railroads, not exceeding the sum of three hundred million dollars. Any indebtedness thereafter contracted in excess of such sum for such purposes shall not be so excluded, but this provision shall not be construed to prevent the refunding of any of the indebtedness excluded hereunder.

C. The aggregate of indebtedness initially contracted from time to time after January first, nineteen hundred fifty, for the construction, reconstruction and equipment of city hospitals, not exceeding the sum of one hundred fifty million dollars. Any indebtedness thereafter contracted in excess of such sum for such purposes, other than indebtedness contracted to refund indebtedness excluded pursuant to this paragraph, shall not be so excluded.

D. The aggregate of indebtedness initially contracted from time to time after January first, nineteen hundred fifty-two, for the construction and equipment of new rapid transit railroads, including extensions of and interconnections with and between existing rapid transit railroads or portions thereof, and reconstruction and equipment of existing rapid transit railroads, not exceeding the sum of five hundred million dollars. Any indebtedness thereafter contracted in excess of such sum for such purposes, other than indebtedness contracted to refund indebtedness excluded pursuant to this paragraph, shall not be so excluded.

E. Indebtedness contracted for school purposes, evidenced by bonds, to the extent to which state aid for common schools, not exceeding two million five hundred thousand dollars, shall meet the interest and the annual requirements for the amortization and payment of part or all of one or more issues of such bonds. Such exclusion shall be effective only during a fiscal year of the city in which its expense budget provides for the payment of such debt service from such state aid. The legislature shall prescribe by law the manner by which the amount of any such exclusion shall be determined and such indebtedness shall not be excluded hereunder except in accordance with the determination so prescribed. Such law may provide that any such determination shall be conclusive if made or approved by the state comptroller.

Section 7-a. Debt-Incurring Power of New York City; Certain Indebtedness for Railroads and Transit Purposes to Be Excluded
In ascertaining the power of the city of New York to contract indebtedness, in addition to the indebtedness excluded under any other section of this constitution, there shall be excluded:

A. The aggregate of indebtedness initially contracted from time to time by the city for the acquisition of railroads and facilities or properties used in connection therewith or rights therein or securities of corporations owning such railroads, facilities or rights, not exceeding the sum of three hundred fifteen million dollars. Provision for the amortization of such indebtedness shall be made either by the establishment and maintenance of a sinking fund therefore or by annual payment of part thereof, or by both such methods. Any indebtedness thereafter contracted in excess of such sum for such purposes shall not be so excluded, but this provision shall not be construed to prevent the refunding of any such indebtedness.

Notwithstanding any other provision of the constitution, the city is hereby authorized to contract indebtedness for such purposes and to deliver its obligations evidencing such indebtedness to the corporations owning the railroads, facilities, properties or rights acquired, to the holders of securities of such owning corporations, to the holders of securities of corporations holding the securities of such owning corporations, or to the holders of securities to which such acquired railroads, facilities, properties or rights are now subject.

B. Indebtedness contracted by the city for transit purposes, and not otherwise excluded, proportionately to the extent to which the current net revenue received by the city from all railroads and facilities and properties used in connection therewith and rights therein owned by the city and securities of corporations owning such railroads, facilities, properties or rights, owned by the city, shall meet the interest and the annual requirements for the amortization and payment of such non-excluded indebtedness.

In determining whether indebtedness for transit purposes may be excluded under this paragraph of this section, there shall first be deducted from the current net revenue received by the city from such railroads and facilities and properties used in connection therewith and rights therein and securities owned by the city:

(a) an amount equal to the interest and amortization requirements on indebtedness for rapid transit purposes heretofore excluded by order of the appellate division, which exclusion shall not be terminated by or under any provision of this section;

(b) an amount equal to the interest on indebtedness contracted pursuant to this section and of the annual requirements for amortization on any sinking fund bonds and for redemption of any serial bonds evidencing such indebtedness;

(c) an amount equal to the sum of all taxes and bridge tolls accruing to the city in the fiscal year of the city preceding the acquisition of the railroads or facilities or properties or rights therein or securities acquired by the city hereunder, from such railroads, facilities and properties; and

(d) the amount of net operating revenue derived by the city from the independent subway system during such fiscal year. The legislature shall prescribe the method by which and the terms and conditions under which the amount of any indebtedness to be excluded hereunder shall be determined, and no indebtedness shall be excluded except in accordance with the determination so prescribed. The legislature may confer appropriate jurisdiction on the appellate division of the supreme court in the first judicial department for the purpose of determining the amount of any debt to be so excluded.

Section 8. Indebtedness Not to Be Invalidated by Operation of this Article

No indebtedness of a county, city, town, village or school district valid at the time of its inception shall thereafter become invalid by reason of the operation of any of the provisions of this article.

Section 9. When Debt-Incurring Power of Certain Counties Shall Cease

Whenever the boundaries of any city are the same as those of a county, or when any city includes within its boundaries more than one county, the power of any county wholly included within such city to contract indebtedness shall cease, but the indebtedness of such county shall not, for the purposes of this article, be included as a part of the city indebtedness.

Section 10. Limitations on Amount to Be Raised by Real Estate Taxes for Local Purposes; Exceptions

Hereafter, in any county, city, village or school district described in this section, the amount to be raised by tax on real estate in any fiscal year, in addition to providing for the interest on and the principal of all indebtedness, shall not exceed an amount equal to the following percentages of the average full valuation of taxable real estate of such county, city, village or school district, less the amount to be raised by tax on real estate in such year for the payment of the interest on and redemption of certificates or other evidence of indebtedness described in paragraphs A and D of section five of this article, or renewals thereof:

(a) any county, for county purposes, one and one-half per centum; provided, however, that the legislature may prescribe a method by which such limitation may be increased to not to exceed two per centum;

(b) any city of one hundred twenty-five thousand or more inhabitants according to the latest federal census, for city purposes, two per centum;

(c) any city having less than one hundred twenty-five thousand inhabitants according to the latest federal census, for city purposes, two per centum;

(d) any village, for village purposes, two per centum;

(e) Notwithstanding the provisions of sub-paragraphs (a) and (b) of this section, the city of New York and the counties therein, for city and county purposes, a combined total of two and one-half per centum.

The average full valuation of taxable real estate of such county, city, village or school district shall be determined by taking the assessed valuations of taxable real estate on the last completed assessment rolls and the four preceding rolls of such county, city, village or school district, and applying thereto the ratio which such assessed valuation on each of such rolls bears to the full valuation, as determined by the state tax commission or by such other state officer or agency as the legislature shall by law direct. The legislature shall prescribe the manner by which such ratio shall be determined by the state tax commission or by such other state officer or agency.

Nothing contained in this section shall be deemed to restrict the powers granted to the legislature by other provisions of this constitution to further restrict the powers of any county, city, town, village or school district to levy taxes on real estate.

Section 10-a. Application and Use of Revenues: Certain Public Improvements

For the purpose of determining the amount of taxes which may be raised on real estate pursuant to section ten of this article, the revenues received in each fiscal year by any county, city or village from a public improvement or part thereof, or service, owned or rendered by such county, city or village for which bonds or capital notes are issued after January first, nineteen hundred fifty, shall be applied first to the payment of all costs of operation, maintenance and repairs thereof, and then to the payment of the amounts required in such fiscal year to pay the interest on and the amortization of, or payment of, indebtedness contracted for such public improvement or part thereof, or service. The provisions of this section shall not prohibit the use of excess revenues for any lawful county, city or village purpose. The provisions of this section shall not be applicable to a public improvement or part thereof constructed to provide for the supply of water.

Section 11. Taxes for Certain Capital Expenditures to Be Excluded from Tax Limitation

(a) Whenever the city of New York is required by law to pay for all or any part of the cost of capital improvements by direct budgetary appropriation in any fiscal year or by the issuance of certificates or other evidence of indebtedness (except serial bonds of an issue having a maximum maturity of more than two years) to be redeemed in one of the two immediately succeeding fiscal years, taxes required for such appropriation or for the redemption of such certificates or other evidence of indebtedness may be excluded in whole or in part by such city from the tax limitation prescribed by section ten of this article, in which event the total amount so required for such appropriation and for the redemption of such certificates or other evidence of indebtedness shall be deemed to be indebtedness to the same extent and in the same manner as if such amount had been financed through indebtedness payable in equal annual installments over the period of the probable usefulness of such capital improvement, as determined by law. The fiscal officer of such city shall determine the amount to be deemed indebtedness pursuant to this section, and the legislature, in its discretion, may provide that such determination, if approved by the state comptroller, shall be conclusive. Any amounts determined to be deemed indebtedness of any county, city, other than the city of New York, village or school district in accordance with the provisions of this section as in force and effect prior to January first, nineteen hundred fifty-two, shall not be deemed to be indebtedness on and after such date.

(b) Whenever any county, city, other than the city of New York, village or school district which is coterminous with, or partly within, or wholly within, a city having less than one hundred twenty-five thousand inhabitants according to the latest federal census provides by direct budgetary appropriation for any fiscal year for the payment in such fiscal year or in any future fiscal year or years of all or any part of the cost of an object or purpose for which a period of probable usefulness has been determined by law, the taxes required for such appropriation shall be excluded from the tax limitation prescribed by section ten of this article unless the legislature otherwise provides.

Section 12. Powers of Local Governments to Be Restricted Further Limitations on Contracting Local Indebtedness Authorized

It shall be the duty of the legislature, subject to the provisions of this constitution, to restrict the power of taxation, assessment, borrowing money, contracting indebtedness, and loaning the credit of counties, cities, towns and villages, so as to prevent abuses in taxation and assessments and in contracting of indebtedness by them. Nothing in this article shall be construed to prevent the legislature from further restricting the powers herein specified of any county, city, town, village or school district to contract indebtedness or to levy taxes on real estate. The legislature shall not, however, restrict the power to levy taxes on real estate for the payment of interest on or principal of indebtedness theretofore contracted.

ARTICLE IX: LOCAL GOVERNMENTS

Section 1. Bill of Rights for Local Governments

Effective local self-government and intergovernmental cooperation are purposes of the people of the state. In furtherance thereof, local governments shall have the following rights, powers, privileges and immunities in addition to those granted by other provisions of this constitution:

(a) Every local government, except a county wholly included within a city, shall have a legislative body elective by the people thereof. Every local government shall have power to adopt local laws as provided by this article.

(b) All officers of every local government whose election or appointment is not provided for by this constitution shall be elected by the people of the local government, or of some division thereof, or appointed by such officers of the local government as may be provided by law.

(c) Local governments shall have power to agree, as authorized by act of the legislature, with the federal government, a state or one or more other governments within or without the state, to provide cooperatively, jointly or by contract any facility, service, activity or undertaking which each participating local government has the power to provide separately. Each such local government shall have power to apportion its share of the cost thereof upon such portion of its area as may be authorized by act of the legislature.

(d) No local government or any part of the territory thereof shall be annexed to another until the people, if any, of the territory proposed to be annexed shall have consented thereto by majority vote on a referendum and until the governing board of each local government, the area of which is affected, shall have consented thereto upon the basis of a determination that the annexation is in the over-all public interest. The consent of the governing board of a county shall be required only where a boundary of the county is affected. On or before July first, nineteen hundred sixty-four, the legislature shall provide, where such consent of a governing board is not granted, for adjudication and determination, on the law and the facts, in a proceeding initiated in the supreme court, of the issue of whether the annexation is in the over-all public interest.

(e) Local governments shall have power to take by eminent domain private property within their boundaries for public use together with excess land or property but no more than is sufficient to provide for appropriate disposition or use of land or property which abuts on that necessary for such public use, and to sell or lease that not devoted to such use. The legislature may authorize and regulate the exercise of the power of eminent domain and excess condemnation by a local government outside its boundaries.

(f) No local government shall be prohibited by the legislature (1) from making a fair return on the value of the property used and useful in its operation of a gas, electric or water public utility service, over and above costs of operation and maintenance and necessary and proper reserves, in addition to an amount equivalent to taxes which such service, if privately owned, would pay to such local government, or (2) from using such profits for payment of refunds to consumers or for any other lawful purpose.

(g) A local government shall have power to apportion its cost of a governmental service or function upon any portion of its area, as authorized by act of the legislature.

(h) (1) Counties, other than those wholly included within a city, shall be empowered by general law, or by special law enacted upon county request pursuant to section two of this article, to adopt, amend or repeal alternative forms of county government provided by the legislature or to prepare, adopt, amend or repeal alternative forms of their own. Any such form of government or any amendment thereof, by act of the legislature or by local law, may transfer one or more functions or duties of the county or of the cities, towns, villages, districts or other units of government wholly contained in such county to each other or when authorized by the legislature to the state, or may abolish one or more offices, departments, agencies or units of government provided, however, that no such form or amendment, except as provided in paragraph (2) of this subdivision, shall become effective unless approved on a referendum by a majority of the votes cast thereon in the area of the county outside of cities, and in the cities of the county, if any, considered as one unit. Where an alternative form of county government or any amendment thereof, by act of the legislature or by local law, provides for the transfer of any function or duty to or from any village or the abolition of any office, department, agency or unit of government of a village wholly contained in such county, such form or amendment shall not become effective unless it shall also be approved on the referendum by a majority of the votes cast thereon in all the villages so affected considered as one unit.

(2) After the adoption of an alternative form of county government by a county, any amendment thereof by act of the legislature or by local law which abolishes or creates an elective county office, changes the voting or veto power of or the method of removing an elective county officer during his or her term of office, abolishes, curtails or transfers to another county officer or agency any power of an elective county officer or changes the form or composition of the county legislative body shall be subject to a permissive referendum as provided by the legislature.

Section 2. Powers and Duties of Legislature; Home Rule Powers of Local Governments; Statute of Local Governments

(a) The legislature shall provide for the creation and organization of local governments in such manner as shall secure to them the rights, powers, privileges and immunities granted to them by this constitution.

(b) Subject to the bill of rights of local governments and other applicable provisions of this constitution, the legislature:

(1) Shall enact, and may from time to time amend, a statute of local governments granting to local governments powers including but not limited to those of local legislation and administration in addition to the powers vested in them by this article. A power granted in such statute may be repealed, diminished, impaired or suspended only by enactment of a statute by the legislature with the approval of the governor at its regular session in one calendar year and the re-enactment and approval of such statute in the following calendar year.

(2) Shall have the power to act in relation to the property, affairs or government of any local government only by general law, or by special law only (a) on request of two-thirds of the total membership of its legislative body or on request of its chief executive officer concurred in by a majority of such membership, or (b) except in the case of the city of New York, on certificate of necessity from the governor reciting facts which in the judgment of the governor constitute an emergency requiring enactment of such law and, in such latter case, with the concurrence of two-thirds of the members elected to each house of the legislature.

(3) Shall have the power to confer on local governments powers not relating to their property, affairs or government including but not limited to those of local legislation and administration, in addition to those otherwise granted by or pursuant to this article, and to withdraw or restrict such additional powers.

(c) In addition to powers granted in the statute of local governments or any other law, (i) every local government shall have power to adopt and amend local laws not inconsistent with the provisions of this constitution or any general law relating to its property, affairs or government and, (ii) every local government shall have power to adopt and amend local laws not inconsistent with the provisions of this constitution or any general law relating to the following subjects, whether or not they relate to the property, affairs or government of such local government, except to the extent that the legislature shall restrict the adoption of such a local law relating to other than the property, affairs or government of such local government:

(I) The powers, duties, qualifications, number, mode of selection and removal, terms of office, compensation, hours of work, protection, welfare and safety of its officers and employees, except that cities and towns shall not have such power with respect to members of the legislative body of the county in their capacities as county officers.

(2) In the case of a city, town or village, the membership and composition of its legislative body.

(3) The transaction of its business.

(4) The incurring of its obligations, except that local laws relating to financing by the issuance of evidences of indebtedness by such local government shall be consistent with laws enacted by the legislature.

(5) The presentation, ascertainment and discharge of claims against it.

(6) The acquisition, care, management and use of its highways, roads, streets, avenues and property.

(7) The acquisition of its transit facilities and the ownership and operation thereof.

(8) The levy, collection and administration of local taxes authorized by the legislature and of assessments for local improvements, consistent with laws enacted by the legislature.

(9) The wages or salaries, the hours of work or labor, and the protection, welfare and safety of persons employed by any contractor or sub-contractor performing work, labor or services for it.

(10) The government, protection, order, conduct, safety, health and well-being of persons or property therein.

(d) Except in the case of a transfer of functions under an alternative form of county government, a local government shall not have power to adopt local laws which impair the powers of any other local government.

(e) The rights and powers of local governments specified in this section insofar as applicable to any county within the city of New York shall be vested in such city.

Section 3. Existing Laws to Remain Applicable; Construction; Definitions

(a) Except as expressly provided, nothing in this article shall restrict or impair any power of the legislature in relation to:

(1) The maintenance, support or administration of the public school system, as required or provided by article XI of this constitution, or any retirement system pertaining to such public school system,

(2) The courts as required or provided by article VI of this constitution, and

(3) Matters other than the property, affairs or government of a local government.

(b) The provisions of this article shall not affect any existing valid provisions of acts of the legislature or of local legislation and such provisions shall continue in force until repealed, amended, modified or superseded in accordance with the provisions of this constitution.

(c) Rights, powers, privileges and immunities granted to local governments by this article shall be liberally construed.

(d) Whenever used in this article the following terms shall mean or include:

(1) "General law." A law which in terms and in effect applies alike to all counties, all counties other than those wholly included within a city, all cities, all towns or all villages.

(2) "Local government." A county, city, town or village.

(3) "People." Persons entitled to vote as provided in section one of article two of this constitution.

(4) "Special law." A law which in terms and in effect applies to one or more, but not all, counties, counties other than those wholly included within a city, cities, towns or villages.

ARTICLE X: CORPORATIONS

Section 1. Corporations; Formation of

Corporations may be formed under general law; but shall not be created by special act, except for municipal purposes, and in cases where, in the judgment of the legislature, the objects of the corporation cannot be attained under general laws. All general laws and special acts passed pursuant to this section may be altered from time to time or repealed.

Section 2. Dues of Corporations

Dues from corporations shall be secured by such individual liability of the corporators and other means as may be prescribed by law.

Section 3. Savings Bank Charters; Savings and Loan Association Charters; Special Charters Not to Be Granted

The legislature shall, by general law, conform all charters of savings banks, savings and loan associations, or institutions for savings, to a uniformity of powers, rights and liabilities, and all charters hereafter granted for such corporations shall be made to conform to such general law, and to such amendments as may be made thereto. The legislature shall have no power to pass any act granting any special charter for banking purposes; but corporations or associations may be formed for such purposes under general laws.

Section 4. Corporations; Definition; Right to Sue and Be Sued

The term corporations as used in this section, and in sections 1, 2 and 3 of this article shall be construed to include all associations and joint-stock companies having any of the powers or privileges of corporations not possessed by individuals or partnerships. And all corporations shall have the right to sue and shall be subject to be sued in all courts in like cases as natural persons.

Section 5. Public Corporations; Restrictions on Creation and Powers; Accounts; Obligations of

No public corporation (other than a county, city, town, village, school district or fire district or an improvement district established in a town or towns) possessing both the power to contract indebtedness and the power to collect rentals, charges, rates or fees for the services or facilities furnished or supplied by it shall hereafter be created except by special act of the legislature.

No such public corporation (other than a county or city) shall hereafter be given both the power to contract indebtedness and the power, within any city, to collect rentals, charges, rates or fees from the owners of real estate, or the occupants of real estate (other than the occupants of premises owned or controlled by such corporation or by the state or any civil division thereof), for services or facilities furnished or supplied in connection with such real estate, if such services or facilities are of a character or nature then or formerly furnished or supplied by the city, unless the electors of the city shall approve the granting to such corporation of such powers by a majority vote at a general or special election in such city; but this paragraph shall not apply to a corporation created pursuant to an interstate compact.

The accounts of every such public corporation heretofore or hereafter created shall be subject to the supervision of the state comptroller, or, if the member or members of such public corporation are appointed by the mayor of a city, to the supervision of the comptroller of such city; provided, however, that this provision shall not apply to such a public corporation created pursuant to agreement or compact with another state or with a foreign power, except with the consent of the parties to such agreement or compact.

Neither the state nor any political subdivision thereof shall at any time be liable for the payment of any obligations issued by such a public corporation heretofore or hereafter created, nor may the legislature accept, authorize acceptance of or impose such liability upon the state or any political subdivision thereof; but the state or a political subdivision thereof may, if authorized by the legislature, acquire the properties of any such corporation and pay the indebtedness thereof.

Section 6. Liability of State for Payment of Bonds of Public Corporation to Construct State Thruways; Use of State Canal Lands and Properties

Notwithstanding any provision of this or any other article of this constitution, the legislature may by law, which shall take effect without submission to the people:

(a) make or authorize making the state liable for the payment of the principal of and interest on bonds of a public corporation created to construct state thruways, in a principal amount not to exceed five hundred million dollars, maturing in not to exceed forty years after their respective dates, and for the payment of the principal of and interest on notes of such corporation issued in anticipation of such bonds, which notes and any renewals thereof shall mature within five years after the respective dates of such notes; and

(b) authorize the use of any state canal lands and properties by such a public corporation for so long as the law may provide. To the extent payment is not otherwise made or provided for, the provisions of section sixteen of article seven shall apply to the liability of the state incurred pursuant to this section, but the powers conferred by this section shall not be subject to the limitations of this or any other article.

Section 7. Liability of State for Obligations of the Port of New York Authority for Railroad Commuter Cars; Limitations

Notwithstanding any provision of this or any other article of this constitution, the legislature may by law, which shall take effect without submission to the people, make or authorize making the state liable for the payment of the principal of and interest on obligations of the port of New York authority issued pursuant to legislation heretofore or hereafter enacted, to purchase or refinance the purchase of, or to repay advances from this state made for the purpose of purchasing, railroad passenger cars, including self-propelled cars, and locomotives and other rolling stock used in passenger transportation, for the purpose of leasing such cars to any railroad transporting passengers between municipalities in the portion of the port of New York district within the state, the majority of the trackage of which within the port of New York district utilized for the transportation of passengers shall be in the state; provided, however, that the total amount of obligations with respect to which the state may be made liable shall not exceed one hundred million dollars at any time, and that all of such obligations shall be due not later than thirty-five years after the effective date of this section.
To the extent payment is not otherwise made or provided for, the provisions of section sixteen of article seven shall apply to the liability of the state incurred pursuant to this section, but the powers conferred by this section shall not be subject to the limitations of this or any other article.

Section 8. Liability of State on Bonds of a Public Corporation to Finance new Industrial or Manufacturing Plants in Depressed Areas

Notwithstanding any provision of this or any other article of this constitution, the legislature may by law, which shall take effect without submission to the people, make or authorize making the state liable for the payment of the principal of and interest on bonds of a public corporation to be created pursuant to and for the purposes specified in the last paragraph of section eight of article seven of this constitution, maturing in not to exceed thirty years after their respective dates, and for the principal of and interest on notes of such corporation issued in anticipation of such bonds, which notes and any renewals thereof shall mature within seven years after the respective dates of such notes, provided that the aggregate principal amount of such bonds with respect to which the state shall be so liable shall not at any one time exceed nine hundred million dollars, excluding bonds issued to refund outstanding bonds.

ARTICLE XI: EDUCATION

Section 1. Common schools

The legislature shall provide for the maintenance and support of a system of free common schools, wherein all the children of this state may be educated.

Section 2. Regents of the University

The corporation created in the year one thousand seven hundred eighty-four, under the name of The Regents of the University of the State of New York, is hereby continued under the name of The University of the State of New York. It shall be governed and its corporate powers, which may be increased, modified or diminished by the legislature, shall be exercised by not less than nine regents.

Section 3. Use of Public Property or Money in Aid of Denominational Schools Prohibited; Transportation of Children Authorized

Neither the state nor any subdivision thereof, shall use its property or credit or any public money, or authorize or permit either to be used, directly or indirectly, in aid or maintenance, other than for examination or inspection, of any school or institution of learning wholly or in part under the control or direction of any religious denomination, or in which any denominational tenet or doctrine is taught, but the legislature may provide for the transportation of children to and from any school or institution of learning.

ARTICLE XII: DEFENSE

Section 1. Defense; Militia

The defense and protection of the state and of the United States is an obligation of all persons within the state. The legislature shall provide for the discharge of this obligation and for the maintenance and regulation of an organized militia.

ARTICLE XIII: PUBLIC OFFICERS

Section 1. Oath of Office; No Other Test for Public Office

Members of the legislature, and all officers, executive and judicial, except such inferior officers as shall be by law exempted, shall, before they enter on the duties of their respective offices, take and subscribe the following oath or affirmation: "I do solemnly swear (or affirm) that I will support the constitution of the United States, and the constitution of the State of New York, and that I will faithfully discharge the duties of the office of ......, according to the best of my ability;" and no other oath, declaration or test shall be required as a qualification for any office of public trust, except that any committee of a political party may, by rule, provide for equal representation of the sexes on any such committee, and a state convention of a political party, at which candidates for public office are nominated, may, by rule, provide for equal representation of the sexes on any committee of such party.

Section 2. Duration of Term of Office

When the duration of any office is not provided by this constitution it may be declared by law, and if not so declared, such office shall be held during the pleasure of the authority making the appointment.

Section 3. Vacancies in Office; How Filled; Boards of Education

The legislature shall provide for filling vacancies in office, and in case of elective officers, no person appointed to fill a vacancy shall hold his or her office by virtue of such appointment longer than the commencement of the political year next succeeding the first annual election after the happening of the vacancy; provided, however, that nothing contained in this article shall prohibit the filling of vacancies on boards of education, including boards of education of community districts in the city school district of the city of New York, by appointment until the next regular school district election, whether or not such appointment shall extend beyond the thirty-first day of December in any year.

Section 4. Political Year and Legislative Term

The political year and legislative term shall begin on the first day of January; and the legislature shall, every year, assemble on the first Wednesday after the first Monday in January.

Section 5. Removal from Office for Misconduct

Provision shall be made by law for the removal for misconduct or malversation in office of all officers, except judicial, whose powers and duties are not local or legislative and who shall be elected at general elections, and also for supplying vacancies created by such removal.

Section 6. When Office to Be Deemed Vacant; Legislature May Declare

The legislature may declare the cases in which any office shall be deemed vacant when no provision is made for that purpose in this constitution.

Section 7. Compensation of Officers

Each of the state officers named in this constitution shall, during his or her continuance in office, receive a compensation, to be fixed by law, which shall not be increased or diminished during the term for which he or she shall have been elected or appointed; nor shall he or she receive to his or her use any fees or perquisites of office or other compensation.

Section 8. Election and Term of City and Certain County Officers
All elections of city officers, including supervisors, elected in any city or part of a city, and of county officers elected in any county wholly included in a city, except to fill vacancies, shall be held on the Tuesday succeeding the first Monday in November in an odd-

numbered year, and the term of every such officer shall expire at the end of an odd- numbered year. This section shall not apply to elections of any judicial officer.

Section 9, 10, 11.

No sections 9, 10, 11.

Section 12.

No section 12.

Section 13. Law Enforcement and Other Officers

(a) Except in counties in the city of New York and except as authorized in section one of article nine of this constitution, registers in counties having registers shall be chosen by the electors of the respective counties once in every three years and whenever the occurring of vacancies shall require; the sheriff and the clerk of each county shall be chosen by the electors once in every three or four years as the legislature shall direct. Sheriffs shall hold no other office. They may be required by law to renew their security, from time to time; and in default of giving such new security, their offices shall be deemed vacant. The governor may remove any elective sheriff, county clerk, district attorney or register within the term for which he or she shall have been elected; but before so doing the governor shall give to such officer a copy of the charges against him or her and an opportunity of being heard in his or her defense. In each county a district attorney shall be chosen by the electors once in every three or four years as the legislature shall direct. The clerk of each county in the city of New York shall be appointed, and be subject to removal, by the appellate division of the supreme court in the judicial department in which the county is located. In addition to his or her powers and duties as clerk of the supreme court, he or she shall have power to select, draw, summon and empanel grand and petit jurors in the manner and under the conditions now or hereafter prescribed by law, and shall have such other powers and duties as shall be prescribed by the city from time to time by local law.

(b) Any district attorney who shall fail faithfully to prosecute a person charged with the violation in his or her county of any provision of this article which may come to his or her knowledge, shall be removed from office by the governor, after due notice and an opportunity of being heard in his or her defense. The expenses which shall be incurred by any county, in investigating and prosecuting any charge of bribery or attempting to bribe any person holding office under the laws of this state, within such county, or of receiving bribes by any such person in said county, shall be a charge against the state, and their payment by the state shall be provided for by law.

(c) The city of New York is hereby vested with power from time to time to abolish by local law, as defined by the legislature, the office of any county officer within the city other than judges, clerks of counties and district attorneys, and to assign any or all functions of such officers to city officers, courts or clerks of counties, and to prescribe the powers, duties, qualifications, number, mode of selection and removal, terms of office and compensation of the persons holding such offices and the employees therein, and to assign to city officers any powers or duties of clerks of counties not assigned by this constitution. The legislature shall not pass any law affecting any such matters in relation to such offices within the city of New York except on message from the governor declaring that an emergency exists and the concurrent action of two-thirds of the members of each house, except that existing laws regarding each such office shall continue in force, and may be amended or repealed by the legislature as heretofore, until the power herein granted to the city has been exercised with respect to that office. The provisions of article nine shall not prevent the legislature from passing general or special laws prescribing or affecting powers and duties of such city officers or such courts or clerks to whom or which functions of such county officers shall have been so assigned, in so far as such powers or duties embrace subjects not relating to property, affairs or government of such city.

Section 14. Employees of, and Contractors for, the State and Local Governments; Wages, Hours and Other Provisions to Be Regulated by Legislature

The legislature may regulate and fix the wages or salaries and the hours of work or labor, and make provisions for the protection, welfare and safety, of persons employed by the state or by any county, city, town, village or other civil division of the state, or by any contractor or subcontractor performing work, labor or services for the state or for any county, city, town, village or other civil division thereof.

ARTICLE XIV: CONSERVATION

Section 1. Forest Preserve to Be Forever Kept Wild; Authorized Uses and Exceptions

The lands of the state, now owned or hereafter acquired, constituting the forest preserve as now fixed by law, shall be forever kept as wild forest lands. They shall not be leased, sold or exchanged, or be taken by any corporation, public or private, nor shall the timber thereon be sold, removed or destroyed. Nothing herein contained shall prevent the state from constructing, completing and maintaining any highway heretofore specifically authorized by constitutional amendment, nor from constructing and maintaining to federal standards federal aid interstate highway route five hundred two from a point in the vicinity of the city of Glens Falls, thence northerly to the vicinity of the villages of Lake George and Warrensburg, the hamlets of South Horicon and Pottersville and thence northerly in a generally straight line on the west side of Schroon Lake to the vicinity of the hamlet of Schroon, then continuing northerly to the vicinity of Schroon Falls, Schroon River and North Hudson, and to the east of Makomis Mountain, east of the hamlet of New Russia, east of the village of Elizabethtown and continuing northerly in the vicinity of the hamlet of Towers Forge, and east of Poke-O-Moonshine Mountain and continuing northerly to the vicinity of the village of Keeseville and the city of Plattsburgh, all of the aforesaid taking not to exceed a total of three hundred acres of state forest preserve land, nor from constructing and maintaining not more than twenty-five miles of ski trails thirty to two hundred feet wide, together with appurtenances thereto, provided that no more than five miles of such trails shall be in excess of one hundred twenty feet wide, on the north, east and northwest slopes of Whiteface Mountain in Essex county, nor from constructing and maintaining not more than twenty-five miles of ski trails thirty to two hundred feet wide, together with appurtenances thereto, provided that no more than two miles of such trails shall be in excess of one hundred twenty feet wide, on the slopes of Belleayre Mountain in Ulster and Delaware counties and not more than forty miles of ski trails thirty to two hundred feet wide, together with appurtenances thereto, provided that no more than eight miles of such trails shall be in excess of one hundred twenty feet wide, on the slopes of Gore and Pete Gay mountains in Warren county, nor from relocating, reconstructing and maintaining a total of not more than fifty miles of existing state highways for the purpose of eliminating the hazards of dangerous curves and grades, provided a total of no more than four hundred acres of forest preserve land shall be used for such purpose and that no single relocated portion of any highway shall exceed one mile in length. Notwithstanding the foregoing provisions, the state may convey to the village of Saranac Lake ten acres of forest preserve land adjacent to the boundaries of such village for public use in providing for refuse disposal and in exchange therefore the village of Saranac Lake shall convey to the state thirty acres of certain true forest land owned by such village on Roaring Brook in the northern half of Lot 113, Township 11, Richards Survey. Notwithstanding the foregoing provisions, the state may convey to the town of Arietta twenty-eight acres of forest preserve land within such town for public use in providing for the extension of the runway and landing strip of the Piseco airport and in exchange therefore the town of Arietta shall convey to the state thirty acres of certain land owned by such town in the town of Arietta. Notwithstanding the foregoing provisions and subject to legislative approval of the tracts to be exchanged prior to the actual transfer of title, the state, in order to consolidate its land holdings for better management, may convey to International Paper Company approximately eight thousand five hundred acres of forest preserve land located in townships two and three of Totten and Crossfield's Purchase and township nine of the Moose River Tract, Hamilton county, and in exchange therefore International Paper Company shall convey to the state for incorporation into the forest preserve approximately the same number of acres of land located within such townships and such County on condition that the legislature shall determine that the lands to be received by the state are at least equal in value to the lands to be conveyed by the state. Notwithstanding the foregoing provisions and subject to legislative approval of the tracts to be exchanged prior to the actual transfer of title and the conditions herein set forth, the state, in order to facilitate the preservation of historic buildings listed on the national register of historic places by rejoining an historic grouping of buildings under unitary ownership and stewardship, may convey to Sagamore Institute, Inc., a not-for-profit educational organization, approximately ten acres of land and buildings thereon adjoining the real property of the Sagamore Institute, Inc. and located on Sagamore Road, near Racquette Lake Village, in the Town of Long Lake, county of Hamilton, and in exchange therefore; Sagamore Institute, Inc. shall convey to the state for incorporation into the forest preserve approximately two hundred acres of wild forest land located within the Adirondack Park on condition that the legislature shall determine that the lands to be received by the state are at least equal in value to the lands and buildings to be conveyed by the state and that the natural and historic character of the lands and buildings conveyed by the state will be secured by appropriate covenants and restrictions and that the lands and buildings conveyed by the state will reasonably be available for public visits according to agreement between Sagamore Institute, Inc. and the state. Notwithstanding the foregoing provisions the state may convey to the town of Arietta fifty acres of forest preserve land within such town for public use in providing for the extension of the runway and landing strip of the Piseco airport and providing for the maintenance of a clear zone around such runway, and in exchange therefore, the town of Arietta shall convey to the state fifty-three acres of true forest land located in lot 2 township 2 Totten and Crossfield's Purchase in the town of Lake Pleasant.

Notwithstanding the foregoing provisions and subject to legislative approval prior to actual transfer of title, the state may convey to the town of Keene, Essex county, for public use as a cemetery owned by such town, approximately twelve acres of forest preserve land within such town and, in exchange therefore, the town of Keene shall convey to the state for incorporation into the forest preserve approximately one hundred forty-four acres of land, together with an easement over land owned by such town including the riverbed adjacent to the land to be conveyed to the state that will restrict further development of such land, on condition that the legislature shall determine that the property to be received by the state is at least equal in value to the land to be conveyed by the state.

Notwithstanding the foregoing provisions and subject to legislative approval prior to actual transfer of title, because there is no viable alternative to using forest preserve lands for the siting of drinking water wells and necessary appurtenances and because such wells are necessary to meet drinking water quality standards, the state may convey to the town of Long Lake, Hamilton county, one acre of forest preserve land within such town for public use as the site of such drinking water wells and necessary appurtenances for the municipal water supply for the hamlet of Raquette Lake. In exchange therefore, the town of Long Lake shall convey to the state at least twelve acres of land located in Hamilton county for incorporation into the forest preserve that the legislature shall determine is at least equal in value to the land to be conveyed by the state. The Raquette Lake surface reservoir shall be abandoned as a drinking water supply source.

Notwithstanding the foregoing provisions and subject to legislative approval prior to actual transfer of title, the state may convey to National Grid up to six acres adjoining State Route 56 in St. Lawrence County where it passes through Forest Preserve in Township 5, Lots 1,2,4 and 6 that is necessary and appropriate for National Grid to construct a new 46kV power line and in exchange therefore National Grid shall convey to the state for incorporation into the forest preserve at least 10 acres of forest land owned by National Grid in St. Lawrence County, on condition that legislature shall determine that the property to be received by the state is at least equal in value to the land conveyed by the state.

Notwithstanding the foregoing provisions, the legislature may authorize the settlement, according to terms determined by the legislature, of title disputes in Township Forty, Totten and Crossfield purchase in the Town of Long Lake, Hamilton County, to resolve longstanding and competing claims of title between the state and private parties in said town- ship, provided that prior to, and as a condition of such settlement, land purchased without the use of state-appropriated funds, and suitable for incorporation in the forest preserve within the Adirondack Park, shall be conveyed to the state on the condition that the legislature shall determine that the property to be conveyed to the state shall provide a net benefit to the forest preserve as compared to the township forty lands subject to such settlement. Notwithstanding the foregoing provisions, the state may authorize NYCO Minerals, Inc. To engage in mineral sampling operations, solely at its expense, to determine the quantity and quality of wollastonite on approximately 200 acres of forest preserve land contained in lot 8, stowers survey, town of lewis, essex county provided that NYCO Minerals, Inc. Shall provide the data and information derived from such drilling to the state for appraisal purposes. Subject to legislative approval of the tracts to be exchanged prior to the actual transfer of title, the state may subsequently convey said lot 8 to NYCO Minerals, Inc., and, in exchange therefor, NYCO Minerals, Inc. Shall convey to the state for incorporation into the forest preserve not less than the same number of acres of land, on condition that the legislature shall determine that the lands to be received by the state are equal to or greater than the value of the land to be conveyed by the state and on condition that the assessed value of the land to be conveyed to the state shall total not less than one million dollars. When NYCO Minerals, Inc. Terminates all mining operations on such lot 8 it shall remediate the site and convey title to such lot back to the state of New York for inclusion in the forest preserve. In the event that lot 8 is not conveyed to NYCO Minerals, Inc. Pursuant to this paragraph, NYCO Minerals, Inc. Nevertheless shall convey to the state for incorporation into the forest preserve not less than the same number of acres of land that is disturbed by any mineral sampling operations conducted on said lot 8 pursuant to this paragraph on condition that the legislature shall determine that the lands to be received by the state are equal to or greater than the value of the lands disturbed by the mineral sampling operations.

Notwithstanding the foregoing provisions and subject to legislative approval prior to actual transfer of title, a total of no more than two hundred fifty acres of forest preserve land shall be used for the establishment of a health and safety land account. Where no viable alternative exists and other criteria developed by the legislature are satisfied, a town, village or county may apply, pursuant to a process determined by the legislature, to the health and safety land account for projects limited to: address bridge hazards or safety on county highways, and town highways listed on the local highway inventory maintained by the department of transportation, dedicated, and in existence on January first, two thousand fifteen, and annually plowed and regularly maintained; elimination of the hazards of dangerous curves and grades on county highways, and town highways listed on the local highway inventory maintained by the department of transportation, dedicated, and in existence on January first, two thousand fifteen, and annually plowed and regularly maintained; relocation and reconstruction and maintenance of county highways, and town highways listed on the local highway inventory maintained by the department of transportation, dedicated, and in existence on January first, two thousand fifteen and annually plowed and regularly maintained, provided further that no single relocated portion of any such highway shall exceed one mile in length; and water wells and necessary appurtenances when such wells are necessary to meet drinking water quality standards and are located within five hundred thirty feet of state highways, county highways, and town highways listed on the local highway inventory maintained by the department of transportation, dedicated, and in existence on January first, two thousand fifteen, and annually plowed and regularly maintained. As a condition of the creation of such health and safety land account the state shall acquire two hundred fifty acres of land for incorporation into the forest preserve, on condition that the legislature shall approve such lands to be added to the forest preserve.

Section 2. Reservoirs

The legislature may by general laws provide for the use of not exceeding three per centum of such lands for the construction and maintenance of reservoirs for municipal water supply, and for the canals of the state. Such reservoirs shall be constructed, owned and controlled by the state, but such work shall not be undertaken until after the boundaries and high flow lines thereof shall have been accurately surveyed and fixed, and after public notice, hearing and determination that such lands are required for such public use. The expense of any such improvements shall be apportioned on the public and private property and municipalities benefited to the extent of the benefits received. Any such reservoir shall always be operated by the state and the legislature shall provide for a charge upon the property and municipalities benefited for a reasonable return to the state upon the value of the rights and property of the state used and the services of the state rendered, which shall be fixed for terms of not exceeding ten years and be readjustable at the end of any term. Unsanitary conditions shall not be created or continued by any such public works.

Section 3. Forest and Wild Life Conservation; Use or Disposition of Certain Lands Authorized

1. Forest and wild life conservation are hereby declared to be policies of the state. For the purpose of carrying out such policies the legislature may appropriate moneys for the acquisition by the state of land, outside of the Adirondack and Catskill parks as now fixed by law, for the practice of forest or wild life conservation. The prohibitions of section 1 of this article shall not apply to any lands heretofore or hereafter acquired or dedicated for such purposes within the forest preserve counties but outside of the Adirondack and Catskill parks as now fixed by law, except that such lands shall not be leased, sold or exchanged, or be taken by any corporation, public or private.

2. As to any other lands of the state, now owned or hereafter acquired, constituting the forest preserve referred to in section one of this article, but outside of the Adirondack and Catskill parks as now fixed by law, and consisting in any case of not more than one hundred contiguous acres entirely separated from any other portion of the forest preserve, the legislature may by appropriate legislation, notwithstanding the provisions of section one of this article, authorize: (a) the dedication thereof for the practice of forest or wild life conservation; or (b) the use thereof for public recreational or other state purposes or the sale, exchange or other disposition thereof; provided, however, that all moneys derived from the sale or other disposition of any of such lands shall be paid into a special fund of the treasury and be expended only for the acquisition of additional lands for such forest preserve within either such Adirondack or Catskill park.

Section 4. Protection of Natural Resources; Development of Agricultural Lands

The policy of the state shall be to conserve and protect its natural resources and scenic beauty and encourage the development and improvement of its agricultural lands for the production of food and other agricultural products. The legislature, in implementing this policy, shall include adequate provision for the abatement of air and water pollution and of excessive and unnecessary noise, the protection of agricultural lands, wetlands and shorelines, and the development and regulation of water resources. The legislature shall further provide for the acquisition of lands and waters, including improvements thereon and any interest therein, outside the forest preserve counties, and the dedication of properties so acquired or now owned, which because of their natural beauty, wilderness character, or geological, ecological or historical significance, shall be preserved and administered for the use and enjoyment of the people. Properties so dedicated shall constitute the state nature and historical preserve and they shall not be taken or otherwise disposed of except by law enacted by two successive regular sessions of the legislature.

Section 5. Violations of Article; How Restrained

A violation of any of the provisions of this article may be restrained at the suit of the people or, with the consent of the supreme court in appellate division, on notice to the attorney-general at the suit of any citizen.

Section 6.

Where state, county, or town highways listed on the local highway inventory maintained by the department of transportation, dedicated and in existence on January first, two thousand fifteen, and annually plowed and regularly maintained, traverse forest preserve land, public utility lines, limited to electric, telephone, broadband, water or sewer lines as defined in law, may, consistent with standards and requirements set forth in law, and following receipt of all permits or authorizations required by law, be buried or co-located within the widths of such highways as defined in law, and bicycle paths may, consistent with standards and requirements set forth in law, and following receipt of all permits or authorizations required by law, be constructed and maintained within the widths of such highways, as defined in law; provided, however, when no viable alternative exists and when necessary to ensure public health and safety, a stabilization device for an existing utility pole may be located in proximity to the width of the road, as defined in law; provided further, that any co-location, burial, maintenance or construction shall minimize the removal of trees or vegetation and shall not include the construction of any new intrastate natural gas or oil pipelines that have not received all necessary state and local permits and authorizations as of June first, two thousand sixteen.

ARTICLE XV: CANALS

Section 1. Disposition of Canals and Canal Properties Prohibited

The legislature shall not sell, abandon or otherwise dispose of the now existing or future improved barge canal, the divisions of which are the Erie canal, the Oswego canal, the Champlain canal, and the Cayuga and Seneca canals, or of the terminals constructed as part of the barge canal system; nor shall it sell, abandon or otherwise dispose of any portion of the canal system existing prior to the barge canal improvement which portion forms a part of, or functions as a part of, the present barge canal system; but such canals and terminals shall remain the property of the state and under its management and control forever. This prohibition shall not prevent the legislature, by appropriate laws, from authorizing the granting of revocable permits or leases for periods of time as authorized by the legislature for the occupancy or use of such lands or structures.

Section 2. Prohibition Inapplicable to Lands and Properties no Longer Useful; Disposition Authorized

The prohibition of sale, abandonment or other disposition contained in section 1 of this article shall not apply to barge canal lands, barge canal terminals or barge canal terminal lands which have or may become no longer necessary or useful for canal or terminal purposes; nor to any canal lands and appertaining structures constituting the canal system prior to the barge canal improvement which have or may become no longer necessary or useful in conjunction with the now existing barge canal. The legislature may by appropriate legislation authorize the sale, exchange, abandonment or other disposition of any barge canal lands, barge canal terminals, barge canal terminal lands or other canal lands and appertaining structures which have or may become no longer necessary or useful as a part of the barge canal system, as an aid to navigation thereon, or for barge canal terminal purposes.
Amendments

Section 3. Contracts for Work and Materials; Special Revenue Fund

All boats navigating the canals and the owners and masters thereof, shall be subject to such laws and regulations as have been or may hereafter be enacted concerning the navigation of the canals. The legislature shall annually make provision for the expenses of the superintendence and repairs of the canals, and may provide for the improvement of the canals in such manner as shall be provided by law notwithstanding the creation of a special revenue fund as provided in this section. All contracts for work or materials on any canal shall be made with the persons who shall offer to do or provide the same at the lowest responsible price, with adequate security for their performance as provided by law.

All funds that may be derived from any sale or other disposition of any barge canal lands, barge canal terminals, barge canal terminal lands or other canal lands and appertaining structures and any other funds collected for the use of the canals or canal lands shall be paid into a special revenue fund of the treasury. Such funds shall only be expended for the maintenance, construction, reconstruction, development or promotion of the canal, canal lands, or lands adjacent to the canal as provided by law.

Section 4. Lease or Transfer to Federal Government of Barge Canal System Authorized

Notwithstanding the prohibition of sale, abandonment or other disposition contained in section one of this article, the legislature may authorize by law the lease or transfer to the federal government of the barge canal, consisting of the Erie, Oswego, Champlain, Cayuga and Seneca divisions and the barge canal terminals and facilities for purposes of operation, improvement and inclusion in the national system of inland waterways. Such lease or transfer to the federal government for the purposes specified herein may be made upon such terms and conditions as the legislature may determine with or without compensation to the state. Nothing contained herein shall prevent the legislature from providing annual appropriations for the state's share, if any, of the cost of operation, maintenance and improvement of the barge canal, the divisions thereof, terminals and facilities in the event of the transfer of the barge canal in whole to the federal government whether by lease or transfer.

The legislature, in determining the state's share of the annual cost of operation, maintenance and improvement of the barge canal, the several divisions, terminals and facilities, shall give consideration and evaluate the benefits derived from the barge canal for purposes of flood control, conservation and utilization of water resources.

ARTICLE XVI: TAXATION

Section 1. Power of Taxation; Exemptions from Taxation
The power of taxation shall never be surrendered, suspended or contracted away, except as to securities issued for public purposes pursuant to law. Any laws which delegate the taxing power shall specify the types of taxes which may be imposed thereunder and provide for their review.
Exemptions from taxation may be granted only by general laws. Exemptions may be altered or repealed except those exempting real or personal property used exclusively for religious, educational or charitable purposes as defined by law and owned by any corporation or association organized or conducted exclusively for one or more of such purposes and not operating for profit.

Section 2. Assessments for Taxation Purposes

The legislature shall provide for the supervision, review and equalization of assessments for purposes of taxation. Assessments shall in no case exceed full value.

Nothing in this constitution shall be deemed to prevent the legislature from providing for the assessment, levy and collection of village taxes by the taxing authorities of those subdivisions of the state in which the lands comprising the respective villages are located, nor from providing that the respective counties of the state may loan or advance to any village located in whole or in part within such county the amount of any tax which shall have been levied for village purposes upon any lands located within such county and remaining unpaid.

Section 3. Situs of Intangible Personal Property; Taxation of

Moneys, credits, securities and other intangible personal property within the state not employed in carrying on any business therein by the owner shall be deemed to be located at the domicile of the owner for purposes of taxation, and, if held in trust, shall not be deemed to be located in this state for purposes of taxation because of the trustee being domiciled in this state, provided that if no other state has jurisdiction to subject such property held in trust to death taxation, it may be deemed property having a taxable situs within this state for purposes of death taxation. Intangible personal property shall not be taxed ad valorem nor shall any excise tax be levied solely because of the ownership or possession thereof, except that the income therefrom may be taken into consideration in computing any excise tax measured by income generally. Undistributed profits shall not be taxed.

Section 4. Certain Corporations Not to Be Discriminated Against

Where the state has power to tax corporations incorporated under the laws of the United States there shall be no discrimination in the rates and method of taxation between such corporations and other corporations exercising substantially similar functions and engaged in substantially similar business within the state.

Section 5. Compensation of Public Officers and Employees Subject to Taxation

All salaries, wages and other compensation, except pensions, paid to officers and employees of the state and its subdivisions and agencies shall be subject to taxation.

Section 6. Public Improvements or Services; Contract of Indebtedness; Creation of Public Corporations

Notwithstanding any provision of this or any other article of this constitution to the contrary, the legislature may by law authorize a county, city, town or village, or combination thereof acting together, to undertake the development of public improvements or services, including the acquisition of land, for the purpose of redevelopment of economically unproductive, blighted or deteriorated areas and, in furtherance thereof, to contract indebtedness. Any such indebtedness shall be contracted by any such county, city, town or village, or combination thereof acting together, without the pledge of its faith and credit, or the faith and credit of the state, for the payment of the principal thereof and the interest thereon, and such indebtedness may be paid without restriction as to the amount or relative amount of annual installments. The amount of any indebtedness contracted under this section may be excluded in ascertaining the power of such county, city, town or village to contract indebtedness within the provisions of this constitution relating thereto. Any county, city, town or village contracting indebtedness pursuant to this section for redevelopment of an economically unproductive, blighted or deteriorated area shall pledge to the payment thereof that portion of the taxes raised by it on real estate in such area which, in any year, is attributed to the increase in value of taxable real estate resulting from such redevelopment. The legislature may further authorize any county, city, town or village, or combination thereof acting together, to carry out the powers and duties conferred by this section by means of a public corporation created therefore.

ARTICLE XVII: SOCIAL WELFARE

Section 1. Public Relief and Care

The aid, care and support of the needy are public concerns and shall be provided by the state and by such of its subdivisions, and in such manner and by such means, as the legislature may from time to time determine.

Section 2. State Board of Social Welfare; Powers and Duties

The state board of social welfare shall be continued. It shall visit and inspect, or cause to be visited and inspected by members of its staff, all public and private institutions, whether state, county, municipal, incorporated or not incorporated, which are in receipt of public funds and which are of a charitable, eleemosynary, correctional or reformatory character, including all reformatories for juveniles and institutions or agencies exercising custody of dependent, neglected or delinquent children, but excepting state institutions for the education and support of the blind, the deaf and the dumb, and excepting also such institutions as are hereinafter made subject to the visitation and inspection of the department of mental hygiene or the state commission of correction. As to institutions, whether incorporated or not incorporated, having inmates, but not in receipt of public funds, which are of a charitable, eleemosynary, correctional or reformatory character, and agencies, whether incorporated or not incorporated, not in receipt of public funds, which exercise custody of dependent, neglected or delinquent children, the state board of social welfare shall make inspections, or cause inspections to be made by members of its staff, but solely as to matters directly affecting the health, safety, treatment and training of their inmates, or of the children under their custody. Subject to the control of the legislature and pursuant to the procedure prescribed by general law, the state board of social welfare may make rules and regulations, not inconsistent with this constitution, with respect to all of the functions, powers and duties with which the department and the state board of social welfare are herein or shall be charged.

Section 3. Public Health

The protection and promotion of the health of the inhabitants of the state are matters of public concern and provision therefore shall be made by the state and by such of its subdivisions and in such manner, and by such means as the legislature shall from time to time determine.

Section 4. Institutions for Detention of Criminals; Probation; Parole; State Commission of Correction

The care and treatment of persons suffering from mental disorder or defect and the protection of the mental health of the inhabitants of the state may be provided by state and local authorities and in such manner as the legislature may from time to time determine. The head of the department of mental hygiene shall visit and inspect, or cause to be visited and inspected by members of his or her staff, all institutions either public or private used for the care and treatment of persons suffering from mental disorder or defect.

Section 5. Institutions for Detention of Criminals; Probation; Parole; State Commission of Correction

The legislature may provide for the maintenance and support of institutions for the detention of persons charged with or convicted of crime and for systems of probation and parole of persons convicted of crime. There shall be a state commission of correction, which shall visit and inspect or cause to be visited and inspected by members of its staff, all institutions used for the detention of sane adults charged with or convicted of crime.

Section 6. Visitation and Inspection

Visitation and inspection as herein authorized, shall not be exclusive of other visitation and inspection now or hereafter authorized by law.

Section 7. Loans for Hospital Construction

Notwithstanding any other provision of this constitution, the legislature may authorize the state, a municipality or a public corporation acting as an instrumentality of the state or municipality to lend its money or credit to or in aid of any corporation or association, regulated by law as to its charges, profits, dividends, and disposition of its property or franchises, for the purpose of providing such hospital or other facilities for the prevention, diagnosis or treatment of human disease, pain, injury, disability, deformity or physical condition, and for facilities incidental or appurtenant thereto as may be prescribed by law.

ARTICLE XVIII: HOUSING

Section 1. Housing and Nursing Home Accommodations for Persons of Low Income; Slum Clearance

Subject to the provisions of this article, the legislature may provide in such manner, by such means and upon such terms and conditions as it may prescribe for low rent housing and nursing home accommodations for persons of low income as defined by law, or for the clearance, replanning, reconstruction and rehabilitation of substandard and insanitary areas, or for both such purposes, and for recreational and other facilities incidental or appurtenant thereto.

Section 2. Idem; Powers of Legislature in Aid of

For and in aid of such purposes, notwithstanding any provision in any other article of this constitution, but subject to the limitations contained in this article, the legislature may: make or contract to make or authorize to be made or contracted capital or periodic subsidies by the state to any city, town, village, or public corporation, payable only with moneys appropriated therefore from the general fund of the state; authorize any city, town or village to make or contract to make such subsidies to any public corporation, payable only with moneys locally appropriated therefore from the general or other fund available for current expenses of such municipality; authorize the contracting of indebtedness for the purpose of providing moneys out of which it may make or contract to make or authorize to be made or contracted loans by the state to any city, town, village or public corporation; authorize any city, town or village to make or contract to make loans to any public corporation; authorize any city, town or village to guarantee the principal of and interest on, or only the interest on, indebtedness contracted by a public corporation; authorize and provide for loans by the state and authorize loans by any city, town or village to or in aid of corporations regulated by law as to rents, profits, dividends and disposition of their property or franchises and engaged in providing housing facilities or nursing home accommodations; authorize any city, town or village to make loans to the owners of existing multiple dwellings for the rehabilitation and improvement thereof for occupancy by persons of low income as defined by law; grant or authorize tax exemptions in whole or in part, except that no such exemption may be granted or authorized for a period of more than sixty years; authorize cooperation with and the acceptance of aid from the United States; grant the power of eminent domain to any city, town or village, to any public corporation and to any corporation regulated by law as to rents, profits, dividends and disposition of its property or franchises and engaged in providing housing facilities.

As used in this article, the term "public corporation" shall mean any corporate governmental agency (except a county or municipal corporation) organized pursuant to law to accomplish any or all of the purposes specified in this article.

Section 3. Article VII to Apply to State Debts under This Article, with Certain Exceptions; Amortization of State Debts; Capital and Periodic Subsidies

The provisions of article VII, not inconsistent with this article, relating to debts of the state shall apply to all debts contracted by the state for the purpose of providing moneys out of which to make loans pursuant to this article, except (a) that any law or laws authorizing the contracting of such debt, not exceeding in the aggregate three hundred million dollars, shall take effect without submission to the people, and the contracting of a greater amount of debt may not be authorized prior to January first, nineteen hundred forty-two; (b) that any such debt and each portion thereof, except as hereinafter provided, shall be paid in equal annual installments, the first of which shall be payable not more than three years, and the last of which shall be payable not more than fifty years, after such debt or portion thereof shall have been contracted; and (c) that any law authorizing the contracting of such debt may be submitted to the people at a general election, whether or not any other law or bill shall be submitted to be voted for or against at such election. Debts contracted by the state for the purpose of providing money out of which to make loans to or in aid of corporations regulated by law as to rents, profits, dividends and disposition of their property or franchises and engaged in providing housing facilities pursuant to this article may be paid in such manner that the total annual charges required for the payment of principal and interest are approximately equal and constant for the entire period in which any of the bonds issued therefore are outstanding.

Any law authorizing the making of contracts for capital or periodic subsidies to be paid with moneys currently appropriated from the general fund of the state shall take effect without submission to the people, and the amount to be paid under such contracts shall not be included in ascertaining the amount of indebtedness which may be contracted by the state under this article; provided, however,

(a) that such periodic subsidies shall not be paid for a period longer than the life of the projects assisted thereby, but in any event for not more than sixty years;

(b) that no contracts for periodic subsidies shall be entered into in any one year requiring payments aggregating more than one million dollars in any one year; and

(c) that there shall not be outstanding at any one time contracts for periodic subsidies requiring payments exceeding an aggregate of thirty-four million dollars in any one year, unless a law authorizing contracts in excess of such amounts shall have been submitted to and approved by the people at a general election; and any such law may be submitted to the people at a general election, whether or not any other law or bill shall be submitted to be voted for or against at such election.

Section 4. Powers of Cities, Towns and Villages to Contract Indebtedness in Aid of Low Rent Housing and Slum Clearance Projects; Restrictions Thereon

To effectuate any of the purposes of this article, the legislature may authorize any city, town or village to contract indebtedness to an amount which shall not exceed two per centum of the average assessed valuation of the real estate of such city, town or village subject to taxation, as determined by the last completed assessment roll and the four preceding assessment rolls of such city, town or village, for city, town or village taxes prior to the contracting of such indebtedness. In ascertaining the power of a city, or village having a population of five thousand or more as determined by the last federal census, to contract indebtedness pursuant to this article there may be excluded any such indebtedness if the project or projects aided by guarantees representing such indebtedness or by loans for which such indebtedness was contracted shall have yielded during the preceding year net revenue to be determined annually by deducting from the gross revenues, including periodic subsidies therefore, received from such project or projects, all costs of operation, maintenance, repairs and replacements, and the interest on such indebtedness and the amounts required in such year for the payment of such indebtedness; provided that in the case of guarantees such interest and such amounts shall have been paid, and in the case of loans an amount equal to such interest and such amounts shall have been paid to such city or village. The legislature shall prescribe the method by which the amount of any such indebtedness to be excluded shall be determined, and no such indebtedness shall be excluded except in accordance with such determination. The legislature may confer appropriate jurisdiction on the appellate division of the supreme court in the judicial departments in which such cities or villages are located for the purpose of determining the amount of any such indebtedness to be so excluded.

The liability of a city, town or village on account of any contract for capital or periodic subsidies to be paid subsequent to the then current year shall, for the purpose of ascertaining the power of such city, town or village to contract indebtedness, be deemed indebtedness in the amount of the commuted value of the total of such capital or periodic subsidies remaining unpaid, calculated on the basis of an annual interest rate of four per centum. Such periodic subsidies shall not be contracted for a period longer than the life of the projects assisted thereby, and in no event for more than sixty years. Indebtedness contracted pursuant to this article shall be excluded in ascertaining the power of a city or such village otherwise to create indebtedness under any other section of this constitution. Notwithstanding the foregoing the legislature shall not authorize any city or village having a population of five thousand or more to contract indebtedness hereunder in excess of the limitations prescribed by any other article of this constitution unless at the same time it shall by law require such city or village to levy annually a tax or taxes other than an ad valorem tax on real estate to an extent sufficient to provide for the payment of the principal of and interest on any such indebtedness. Nothing herein contained, however, shall be construed to prevent such city or village from pledging its faith and credit for the payment of such principal and interest nor shall any such law prevent recourse to an ad valorem tax on real estate to the extent that revenue derived from such other tax or taxes in any year, together with revenues from the project or projects aided by the proceeds of such indebtedness, shall become insufficient to provide fully for payment of such principal and interest in that year.

Section 5. Liability for Certain Loans Made by the State to Certain Public Corporations

Any city, town or village shall be liable for the repayment of any loans and interest thereon made by the state to any public corporation, acting as an instrumentality of such city, town or village. Such liability of a city, town or village shall be excluded in ascertaining the power of such city, town or village to become indebted pursuant to the provisions of this article, except that in the event of a default in payment under the terms of any such loan, the unpaid balance thereof shall be included in ascertaining the power of such city, town or village to become so indebted. No subsidy, in addition to any capital or periodic subsidy originally contracted for in aid of any project or projects authorized under this article, shall be paid by the state to a city, town, village or public corporation, acting as an instrumentality thereof, for the purpose of enabling such city, town, village or corporation to remedy an actual default or avoid an impending default in the payment of principal or interest on a loan which has been theretofore made by the state to such city, town, village or corporation pursuant to this article.

Section 6. Loans and Subsidies; Restrictions on and Preference in Occupancy of Projects

No loan, or subsidy shall be made by the state to aid any project unless such project is in conformity with a plan or undertaking for the clearance, replanning and reconstruction or rehabilitation of a substandard and unsanitary area or areas and for recreational and other facilities incidental or appurtenant thereto. The legislature may provide additional conditions to the making of such loans or subsidies consistent with the purposes of this article. The occupancy of any such project shall be restricted to persons of low income as defined by law and preference shall be given to persons who live or shall have lived in such area or areas.

Section 7. Liability Arising from Guarantees to Be Deemed Indebtedness; Method of Computing

The liability arising from any guarantee of the principal of and interest on indebtedness contracted by a public corporation shall be deemed indebtedness in the amount of the face value of the principal thereof remaining unpaid. The liability arising from any guarantee of only the interest on indebtedness contracted by a public corporation shall be deemed indebtedness in the amount of the commuted value of the total interest guaranteed and remaining unpaid, calculated on the basis of an annual interest rate of four per centum.

Section 8. Excess Condemnation

Any agency of the state, or any city, town, village, or public corporation, which is empowered by law to take private property by eminent domain for any of the public purposes specified in section one of this article, may be empowered by the legislature to take property necessary for any such purpose but in excess of that required for public use after such purpose shall have been accomplished; and to improve and utilize such excess, wholly or partly for any other public purpose, or to lease or sell such excess with restrictions to preserve and protect such improvement or improvements.

Section 9. Acquisition of Property for Purposes of Article

Subject to any limitation imposed by the legislature, the state, or any city, town, village or public corporation, may acquire by purchase, gift, eminent domain or otherwise, such property as it may deem ultimately necessary or proper to effectuate the purposes of this article, or any of them, although temporarily not required for such purposes.

Section 10. Power of Legislature; Construction of Article

The legislature is empowered to make all laws which it shall deem necessary and proper for carrying into execution the foregoing powers. This article shall be construed as extending powers which otherwise might be limited by other articles of this constitution and shall not be construed as imposing additional limitations; but nothing in this article contained shall be deemed to authorize or empower the state, or any city, town, village or public corporation to engage in any private business or enterprise other than the building and operation of low rent dwelling houses for persons of low income as defined by law, or the loaning of money to owners of existing multiple dwellings as herein provided.

ARTICLE XIX: AMENDMENTS TO CONSTITUTION

Section 1. Amendments to Constitution; How Proposed, Voted upon and Ratified; Failure of Attorney-General to Render Opinion Not to Affect Validity

Any amendment or amendments to this constitution may be proposed in the senate and assembly whereupon such amendment or amendments shall be referred to the attorney-general whose duty it shall be within twenty days thereafter to render an opinion in writing to the senate and assembly as to the effect of such amendment or amendments upon other provisions of the constitution. Upon receiving such opinion, if the amendment or amendments as proposed or as amended shall be agreed to by a majority of the members elected to each of the two houses, such proposed amendment or amendments shall be entered on their journals, and the ayes and noes taken thereon, and referred to the next regular legislative session convening after the succeeding general election of members of the assembly, and shall be published for three months previous to the time of making such choice; and if in such legislative session, such proposed amendment or amendments shall be agreed to by a majority of all the members elected to each house, then it shall be the duty of the legislature to submit each proposed amendment or amendments to the people for approval in such manner and at such times as the legislature shall prescribe; and if the people shall approve and ratify such amendment or amendments by a majority of the electors voting thereon, such amendment or amendments shall become a part of the constitution on the first day of January next after such approval. Neither the failure of the attorney-general to render an opinion concerning such a proposed amendment nor his or her failure to do so timely shall affect the validity of such proposed amendment or legislative action thereon.

Section 2. Future Constitutional Conventions; How Called; Election of Delegates; Compensation; Quorum; Submission of Amendments; Officers; Employees; Rules; Vacancies

At the general election to be held in the year nineteen hundred fifty-seven, and every twentieth year thereafter, and also at such times as the legislature may by law provide, the question "Shall there be a convention to revise the constitution and amend the same?" shall be submitted to and decided by the electors of the state; and in case a majority of the electors voting thereon shall decide in favor of a convention for such purpose, the electors of every senate district of the state, as then organized, shall elect three delegates at the next ensuing general election, and the electors of the state voting at the same election shall elect fifteen delegates-at-large. The delegates so elected shall convene at the capitol on the first Tuesday of April next ensuing after their election, and shall continue their session until the business of such convention shall have been completed. Every delegate shall receive for his or her services the same compensation as shall then be annually payable to the members of the assembly and be reimbursed for actual traveling expenses, while the convention is in session, to the extent that a member of the assembly would then be entitled thereto in the case of a session of the legislature. A majority of the convention shall constitute a quorum for the transaction of business, and no amendment to the constitution shall be submitted for approval to the electors as hereinafter provided, unless by the assent of a majority of all the delegates elected to the convention, the ayes and noes being entered on the journal to be kept. The convention shall have the power to appoint such officers, employees and assistants as it may deem necessary, and fix their compensation and to provide for the printing of its documents, journal, proceedings and other expenses of said convention. The convention shall determine the rules of its own proceedings, choose its own officers, and be the judge of the election, returns and qualifications of its members. In case of a vacancy, by death, resignation or other cause, of any district delegate elected to the convention, such vacancy shall be filled by a vote of the remaining delegates representing the district in which such vacancy occurs. If such vacancy occurs in the office of a delegate-at-large, such vacancy shall be filled by a vote of the remaining delegates-at-large. Any proposed constitution or constitutional amendment which shall have been adopted by such convention, shall be submitted to a vote of the electors of the state at the time and in the manner provided by such convention, at an election which shall be held not less than six weeks after the adjournment of such convention. Upon the approval of such constitution or constitutional amendments, in the manner provided in the last preceding section, such constitution or constitutional amendment, shall go into effect on the first day of January next after such approval.

Section 3. Amendments Simultaneously Submitted by Convention and Legislature

Any amendment proposed by a constitutional convention relating to the same subject as an amendment proposed by the legislature, coincidentally submitted to the people for approval shall, if approved, be deemed to supersede the amendment so proposed by the legislature.

ARTICLE XX: WHEN TO TAKE EFFECT

Section 1. This constitution shall be in force from and including the first day of January, one thousand nine hundred thirty-nine, except as herein otherwise provided.

Closing

Done in Convention at the Capitol in the city of Albany, the twenty-fifth day of August, in the year one thousand nine hundred thirty- eight, and of the Independence of the United States of America the one hundred and sixty-third.

In witness whereof, we have hereunto subscribed our names.

Frederick E. Crane, President and Delegate-at-Large

U.H. Boyden, Secretary

www.ingramcontent.com/pod-product-compliance
Lightning Source LLC
Chambersburg PA
CBHW052314220526
45472CB00001B/107